WRITING—
BY COINCIDENCE

WRITING—
BY COINCIDENCE

Flowing with Signs & Synchronicities to Write with Passion

Jenna Moore Fuller

WRITING—BY COINCIDENCE

Flowing with Signs & Synchronicities to Write with Passion

Also by Jenna Moore Fuller

The Secret Language of Synchronicity:
Deciphering the Words & Wisdom of Meaningful Coincidence

For all my O-D-D Explorers, who helped me follow the clues;
and of course the big U for providing them.

CONTENTS

INTRODUCTION

January, Salem, OR: Something odd had happened. By odd I don't mean creepy weird, but mysterious instead. And totally out-of-the-blue unexpected. In fact, the surprise of it made me a bit shaky, so I sat down to think it over, and plan where to go from there. All with a goofy smile still on my face. Here's what went on.

I wanted to write another book. My first book about coincidence, was out and being read, so things were good there. Its theme, following signs and synchronicities, was my thing—that I aimed to live and explore—and that's exactly what happened here. I had learned to write about what I felt most about, through the flow of meaningful messages; and that's what I wanted to share.

It was a strange concept. I mean, how many people wanting to write would think of coincidence? And be open to the idea of its helpful role? Intuitive writing was one thing—we're all pretty much aware of the value of insights—but following signs? Just thinking about how that might be viewed made me nervous.

So I did what works well with questions that are big and need tending to: mentally "asked" and put that out there to the ethers, saying something like, "Should I write a book about writing with the help of coincidence?" Then I put the whole thing aside and got on with my day.

But not too much. A few minutes later, I started looking for an article I'd once read. As I pulled a few magazines from a shelf, a small scrap of paper fell out of the pages and fluttered to the floor. I picked it up and started, for what was written there seemed a message just for me. "Let's!" was all the paper said.

My heart did a sort of skip-a-beat, for here was my answer! Delivered by coincidence, no less. But what did it mean but a confirmation of some sort? Oh, of course: let's, as in more than just me; let us write this book together. Together, as in the Universe and me. That part of the message was totally clear.

But there was a mystery. The handwriting was familiar and obviously mine! But when did I write it and why? And how did it happen to end up here, right now, as an answer for me? This part felt enjoyably eerie, and I gave it some thought, coming up without much at all.

I did vaguely remember a note about an outing some time before. Could that be the source of the paper? Maybe. But if so, it didn't matter now. I'd received a message that felt right and true, and helped me know what I really wanted to do. You bet, I thought to myself, let's write it!

But wait—why writing by coincidence? What's the point of those two things combined? And how do our passions fit in? Because coincidence is the forgotten part of guidance, conveyed as answers and outer clues. And so it plays a fantastic role in our goal to write what we feel.

This book has two main sections. Part I covers the background of coincidence, and Part II the process of writing in the flow of its help. The whole thing is a mix of discoveries and ideas and stories of my own synchronistic events that happened *while* I was writing, and those of some others that also tied in.

My goals here were simple: To share my experience of writing with the help of coincidence. To inspire your desire to write what you feel. And for both of us to enjoy the adventure. For this book was written as it reads, in the flow of meaningful messages which went to places mysterious and new. I hope you'll come along with me for the coincidental ride!

PART I

1: BASICS OF COINCIDENCE

So what is meaningful coincidence anyway? Many people had probably never heard of Swiss psychologist Carl Jung or his "synchronicity" research back in the 1930s, but were aware of odd instances of it happening to them. Synchronicity, or meaningful coincidence for Jung, was when events occurred simultaneously but not as cause and effect. It often consisted of inner and outer experiences somehow linked, but not causally, and which felt significant to the recipient.

Pretty much any inner state can trigger coincidence: thoughts, ideas, feelings, or dreams. Somehow these states naturally join up with outer things, as answering information and events. Common examples are the times we focus on something physical we want that quickly shows up in or world, or think about someone who then contacts us or appears.

Some of the most intriguing instances involve coincidental messages; the exact information or solution needed. We might, for instance, hear a conversation, receive a letter, or find a new book. The message conveyed in each case will perfectly fit our wants. I once had a conversation with a friend about ultimate good health. What are the top things, we wondered, that a person can do? The next day while browsing in a shop I came upon an unknown book whose description included our question, nearly word for word. Talk about a fast response!

Another time my husband and I were on the freeway discussing where to stop for lunch. "Sweet Tomatoes?" Eric asked, referring to a well-known restaurant in the area. Immediately, as if on cue, a big truck with an ad featuring a large, luscious-looking tomato passed by. Quick confirmation on that one for sure.

On another occasion I was riding with a relative on a day-trip to Washington State. She was talking about visiting a friend the next day. Right then a sign for some little town named the same as her friend popped up on the side of the road. "That is a good idea," it seemed to say.

So what do these cases of coincidence have in common? Some kind of basic inherent laws? And do they explain why it happens at all? Let's take a closer look at the likelihood of this idea.

The Why

Most of us are curious about why some things happen. With meaningful coincidence it is a challenge to know. Because reality is linked to personal feelings, and to significance that's personal too. But by observing our own incidents, we are able to see what's there: synchronicity, real and true. And that probably is the only way to really know it.

The same applies to its workings. Being subjective, no set explanation of how coincidence operates is possible. Its reality can only be proven in the private lives of its recipients. Even so, my personal experiences, plus the synchronicities of others, point to some premises that feel positively good. The experiences of many of us suggest:

Our Universe is responsive and wise. It reacts to our needs and desires through the "asking" of our thoughts. A higher force more knowing and powerful than us helps us through coincidental messages and events. We are never alone, it appears, whatever happens.

This Cosmos is connected and arranged. Our lives appear to be directed by designs of association and order, their incidents well-orchestrated and joined. Individuals' inner and outer states are somehow united with no separation between mental and physical experiences. Life, it seems, in all its intricacy, is completely linked.

A couple images this morning reinforced these insights on connections. I was on my way to the library. A truck in front of me carrying office supplies pictured giant balls of rubber bands on its panels. It was an attention-catching ad, with the multi-colored bands wound around the balls and crisscrossing each other. They were separate yet linked—like our personal lives, and our inner and outer states as well.

Then at the library, a knitting book was displayed above the new non-fiction shelves. Its cover pictured another ball, this time wound with yarn, which again reminded me of our common threads. Separate yet joined, our experiences and our lives, and also one another; a helpful thing about coincidence we might remember.

Things happen for a reason. Though they sometimes are mysterious, there's meaning behind them all through the muse and messages we receive. What seems like happenchance is part of the magic act. And we're its subject.

Synchronicity seems part of a personal plan for our blossoming and well-being, as a secret path to our best and most flourishing self. This guidance toward highest good is conveyed through our coincidences, in a variety of surprising forms. Chosen and conveyed to us as that moment's best fit.

As I wrote those last words I had a flash about something strange. Nothing huge or anything—just something a little odd—that completely caught me off-guard, yet carried a message.

May, Salem, OR: I was driving with Eric. We were talking about our plans for day when he turned and out of nowhere asked me, "What color is your fortune cookie?"

"Huh?" I answered.

"What color is your fortune cookie?" he repeated.

"What are you talking about?"

"I have no idea," he replied. "It just came into my head."

"Oh, okay." Playing along now, I thought about this for a minute or two. "Mine is pale yellow. It's a new day and the light is clear and promising. Hey, I'm not really sure what I am saying either, but that idea quickly came out. What color is your fortune cookie?"

"Dark green," he said. "I didn't sleep as well as usual last night." And that was the end of that.

But what had happened there?

Eric is artistic in an earthy sort of way. He designs and builds a great many things. He photographs flowers and loves their colorful shades. But he doesn't talk in metaphors as a rule.

Yet I do, now and then, as my mind tends that way, and thinks that way a lot. So the cookie as a symbol made good sense to me. What was surprising, though, was hearing it from Eric. It felt like a best-fit message for this book and our benefit here. That showed up, as usual, by coincidence.

The How

Law of attraction. Most of us are somewhat familiar with this recently popular term, referring to the concept of like attracting like. More precisely, that our thoughts attract similar things, like events and information. This idea has been around for a very long time. Current studies in science are starting to confirm what many of us already knew—that our minds make stuff happen!

The implications of this are huge. If our inner thoughts trigger outer answers and events, we actually do create our own reality. To a mind-boggling extent anyway. Though the characteristics of the answers are as varied as our thoughts, their basic form is not. Synchronicities respond to our asking with coincidental help.

This linking of an inner and outer experience always relates to our focus. We send out signals with our strongest thoughts. And when we do, answers will come through messages and events. Bu here's the catch: we'll only benefit from them if we recognize them, by being open and aware.

Synchronicities often follow a common sequence: the asking followed by an intuition, then a coincidence. Our focus triggers an inner urge to do something or go somewhere. If we follow these urges, helpful messages or circumstances will appear.

I once had a dream that felt like higher guidance on this very thing. In it, I was shown through moving pictures how reality changes depending on our dominant thoughts.

The Who

Does everyone have synchronicities? Or only an enlightened few? Though it is impossible to know for sure, probably everyone. An exception might be those who have trouble focusing, but who is really to know? What feels meaningful to each of us is personal.

If most of have them, then why aren't we aware of them if they're unusual or odd? "Awareness" is probably our key word here. We must know they exist to see them, and their significance to read them, and to really care. So it gets down to being open and alert.

And do we play the same part in every coincidence? As the star, the only role, in our uncanny show? Not hardly. Sometimes it takes a whole cast of supporting characters to play out. Then there are times we're part of the incidents of others; from bit player to major role, apparently depending on the recipient's needs. With the big U directing, of course!

The When

Timing is everything to coincidence. There's a meeting of events, inner and outer, at just the right moment for us. Synchronicities, it's evident, are wisely arranged to be pertinent and precise. Timing is everything.

The moment a synchronicity happens depends on our needs. There's a coming together of answering things. Whatever question or desire we're focused upon will trigger the response. This may be information or circumstances, like people, places, and things; whatever elements are necessary. Whenever an incident happens, we'll likely be awed as well, by the coincidental, pitch-perfect timing of it all.

May, Keizer, OR: It was morning, the next day after I finished writing this section. Maybe. The thought had been going through my mind as I had written the last part that a new example would be welcome, if it occurred.

I received an email from my friend Amy. It was one of those albums of fascinating photos that appear from time to time. This one of beautiful world views featured rare scenes of nature that were simply awesome.

There were strange rainbows of sparkles and mist that danced and twirled. Clouds in the shape of angels and waves. An underwater magical place with a divers' resting bench. There were crystals and ice, carved and natural, set in surreal scenes. Flourishing flowers in proud profusion. And yet, those few special places were just a smattering.

The meaning of the show to me was pure potential. "Look at

this," it seemed to say, "look at what we can do! And in whatever color or shape or pattern works for you. And likewise our messages. Designed and delivered in endless forms, through coincidence."

2: BENEFITS OF COINCIDENCE

What's the big deal with coincidence anyway? Is it really that important? And why do we need to know about it to write? Well, we don't really. With practice and persistence we can be good writers, after all. But with higher guidance we can literally shine. And that guidance often comes through coincidence.

Along with the advantage of help with our writing are some other awesome benefits of being in the know and Universal flow. Here are the three biggies from my experience that can boggle our minds and inspire lives—by chance.

Connection

Coincidence shows us our world is joined, things connected in some sort of way. This includes everything: people, objects, places, circumstances, etc. Our focus on questions results in links that offer the answers we need. All seemingly by coincidence, of course.

August, Keizer, OR: My friend Lisa and I were going out to lunch. Before leaving, she handed me a newspaper page. "This is a really fun story, and I knew you would like to read," she said, "about a bunch of old letters that were found in a trunk, and made their way back to an ancestor of the letters' recipient—

finally."

Indeed, I did want to read it. Lisa knew of my fascination and involvement with letters from the past.

Later I did, and it was a curious tale. Turned out that by coincidence the finder of the letters had once worked in the same place as a relative of their recipient. In time the old letters, somehow once lost, were back with a member of their own family, who was delighted and amazed. No big deal, it seems for the Universe, and happy to oblige!

Meaningful coincidence connects us with that creative force as well. What a wonderful feeling it is to know we're not alone; that the Universe is there for us! That we can reach out and connect to its support whenever we want. And especially consoling during those extra solitary spells, when everything is just too quiet.

June, Keizer, OR: It was a beautiful day outside. The sky was crystal blue, the air soft and warm, but somewhat lost on me. I was trying to work, but felt a bit off. The thing, it seemed, was the quiet. I was at home alone and no one was around. And that just didn't feel right.

Often it did. Sometimes a quiet spell to work was just what I craved and needed. But occasionally it was too, well, quiet and isolating! I knew that this was what was up this time. Too far away from other writers who liked the same things as me.

I had good friends, of course that I cared about, to spend time with. And for that was glad and grateful. And sometimes I worked near library writers too. But I missed talking with others who wrote, about the nature of our craft. Talks that were warm, fun, and helpful to each other.

So I decided to go out for a while and do a little browsing; change my surroundings and my view. And as often happens, going to a thrift store was what sounded good. As I headed out I made a note to be open and alert for anything unusual that might have to do with our topic here.

Once inside the store I started looking at some decorative items. On the top shelf of the aisle, an attractive box stood out. I took it down to look closer. It was a wooden box for tea, partitioned inside for storage. The cover was striking, with carved images of a teapot, cups, and the word "TEA." Borders of the lid were decorated with a swirling design of orange, blue, and gold.

I liked the box. It made me think of pleasant rituals and respect for things we love, and comfy conversations over cookies and tea. It was just a pretty box, but it reminded me in a roundabout way of what I'd been missing: the camaraderie of fellow authors.

I looked at other items on the nearby shelves. There was a small teapot for sale that looked almost like the design on the box, with the same colors and shape. That was strange. Another reference to tea that caught my attention. But maybe not so unusual. Didn't most teapots look pretty much the same?

No, that wasn't true. Though never much of a tea drinker, I knew through observation that ceramics and kitchenware varied a great deal from one piece to another. Feeling a little curious now, I took a look at some teapots in another part of the store, noting how each was quite different than the image on the box. Hmmm.

Over in the aisles of books for sale, I took a look at the self-help section. The title of one book seemed to jump right out, with its theme of friendship, and its illustrations of tea. This was a little confusing. I had no doubt that there was something going on; those references to tea were too obvious.

Yet I didn't have that sense of knowing they were signs. Maybe it was just selective observation on my part about some common objects and words? If they were meant as a message for me, I needed something more.

I finished my shopping and went to the car. Before leaving I checked my email. There was a note from Deidre in which she mentioned disliking the stories of an author's books. "Not my cut of tea," she concluded. Voila! A little thrill ran through me as I recognized the message repeated once more, through the wording and symbol of tea. But what was the meaning of that message?

Thinking it all over, I was surprised and humbled by the answer that came. For that comfy cup of tea was my perfect symbol! What was awesome was that I had never thought of it, consciously anyway, until then. But nonetheless, an image was offered to help me remember what I knew down deep: that the big U is our companion, whenever we wish; we are never really alone. That it's caring and encouraging and funny too. That, like a cozy talk over tea with a friend, it's there when we need it, with heartfelt support and opinions.

And a side note: there's often a surprise element of coincidence. We can welcome it, and study it, but never predict it, for it brings cosmic answers after all.

Like with this incident, I had always been intrigued by the concept of English tea. I had read about it in lots and lots of novels, plus my bookseller background too, and wondered about it (all those Croxton, Dimmick, and Moore ancestors), but never explored it further. Yet when used as a symbol, its meaning clearly came through in a personal, colorful, and surprising way.

Answers are another part of coincidental connection. When we pay attention to those events, responses are seen. These will be in one or a combination of two forms; information or materializations. Informative answers include all the various kinds of messages that coincidentally reply to our questions and concerns. These may be big solutions and new ideas, or confirmation of our course. Or quick bits of info about minor things. Either way, the answers received seemingly by chance are apt and personal.

Materializations occur as the result of our focus. These answer our wants and our needs. Objects and circumstances or both just happen to appear. These can be so much fun to see! The big U's conjuring presents some surprising shows, and we benefit from its magic. Its aim, after all, is to please.

August, Corrales, NM: Deidre sent me this email. "Ready for a fun coincidence? OK. Yesterday I mentioned yoga nidra meditation to you. This morning on our walk, Lorraine said, 'I know you meditate. A friend of mine in Oregon sent me a yoga nidra meditation CD. Would you like to borrow it?' All I could say was, 'Wow! I have been thinking about looking into that!' So I have the CD, and will see what the deal is."

As writers, this connection via coincidence can help us cope and thrive, through answers that solve or inspire, plus provide the fun of a friendship—of sorts—that shares and cares.

Now let's look at a second huge benefit of synchronicity.

Meaning

Coincidence shows us that our lives are important. Their events are not random, but ordered instead. There is a plan in place behind what happens for us. When we follow the clues of coincidence, this purpose becomes clearer. Our work, our play—our whole lives do matter! Synchronicity carries meaningful messages for our highest and happiest selves.

Two minutes ago, August, Keizer, OR: I finished writing the last paragraph. Then thought to myself, I wish I had a story for this part about meaning. But I didn't, and felt like taking a break on the deck. I went out, and the weather was perfect. After the last few scorcher days, the air was warm with just a hint of breeze. I took a seat to enjoy the view and also check my mail.

There was a note from Deidre which began, "I like the story of your mom's caregiver and the sketch book. It's a nice story for you as well as your mom."

What? The wording caught me by surprise, and then sent a little zip through my mind. A story for me as well? Oh! Of course, for us here. And I had forgotten all about it until then. But it reminded then, by chance, that really wasn't at all. Here is the story.

When I visited my parents the other day I saw something new, a sketchbook on the table. Its cover was decorated with "Tommie", Mom's name, and sparkly stick-on flowers. Inside was a handwritten note. The note explained how the writer had always enjoyed looking at Tommie's artwork when she came into her rooms, how she had asked her how long it had been since she'd painted, and that the answer had been "ages."

So, the writer went on, here was a clean new book, just for her to do some sketching. How she hoped that Tommie would try to draw a little bit every day. Because she was creative still, and would probably enjoy it once she began. The note was signed by the caregiver's unusual name, Fate.

This was such a kind thing to do. It was a gesture from the heart that aimed to stir my mom's spirit, her creative passion for art, which she hadn't been physically able to do for awhile. The gift-giver knew it, and was happy to play her part.

But I think it was more than that too. A surprise from Spirit for Tommie to encourage her to try, for the work she loved still mattered: to her for the pleasure, to others for the beauty, and for us, a reminder. Our lives and our work and the whole vast world are intentional.

As writers, this meaningfulness can help us cope and thrive, as does the benefit of connection. Knowing that what we love is our path really changes things. The hard parts aren't so bad, and the easy parts are even better when we know they're part of our plan.

Fulfillment

Coincidence offers us fulfillment in our lives. Incidents occur that lead us to feeling satisfied and complete. Things happening seemingly by chance help us to know who we are and experience our reach. It always feels good to realize our full potential.

August, Lincoln City, OR: We were on our way to the beach. It was hot at home in the valley, but cool at the coast. So we packed up a lunch and headed over. The ocean was only an hour's drive, with plenty of pretty views, and I couldn't wait to get there.

It had always been that way for me: a favorite place I loved to be in most any kind of weather. A place of mesmerizing beauty and joy—and messages. Yet I wasn't sure why the latter was true. There was that urge to leave our mark, of course, for later folks to see. So names and dated appeared on rocks and trees. But words on the beach were different, etched boldly in the sand, before being washed away to sea.

I suspected it had to do with the grandeur of the space. We felt the power of its energy and its everlasting flow. And the joy of that sense reached deep—to our own inner depths—and we stopped to write some words in the sand. Or to read what had been written there by others. There were other messages too at the beach. I had stayed in rooms with happy journals where guests could write. And they had, with page after page of feelings and thoughts about their visits and selves. With clearly honest entries, sharing bits of secrets sometimes, with people unknown.

I once told a story of my own in such a book. It was summer, and we'd been driving on a tourist-packed street a little while before. At a light we stopped along with many other drivers. Then from somewhere on the side a toddler stepped out—and onto the road.

Everything seemed to halt, as the tot wove back and forth through cars, too short to be seen by most. But a woman up front was alert and amazingly fast. Jumping out of her car, she scooped up the child, and dashed to the side of the road, and handed her to Mom standing there, still frozen in fear. Then back to her own car sitting idle in the middle, and off in a flash, as the light turned green.

We drove on, a little shaken, but enlivened too, by the stranger's compassion; her willingness to take that personal risk for the child. It went beyond mere instinct, that I was sure, to who she was inside. And she wasn't afraid to act from that self.

I like to bring a treasure home from the beach; an ocean gem that speaks to me, like a driftwood scrap or polished stone. These may carry messages about my thoughts, so it's fun to collect the clues which can lead to insights and ideas.

The last time there it was a rock. I spotted the stone down close to the crashing waves. It was salty and wet, having just tumbled out of the surf, and it stood out from other sea-washed stones nearby. I knew right away that this was my gem for the day, the one that was meant for me.

It was a lumpish stone, light gray in color, and triangle-shaped. One side of its surface was covered with craters. Each of these was layered with a creamy white mineral of some kind or another. What was unique about it was this layering. Though there were other cratered rocks scattered about, this two-toned one was different.

I picked it up from the beach and washed off the sand, then admired its appeal. It felt a bit mysterious, like a gift from the sea. It also seemed symbolic—though I wasn't sure of what—so I put it in my pocket and walked on.

Later, back home, I studied the rock again, in particular its colored craters, for they were what pulled me in. Something about seeing deeper into the stone. Into its center, past the outer layers, to the best part inside.

Then I got it, and the "Aha" felt sweet: the stone was a confirming sign. Its layered yet open nature was a message for us here. For our lives can be fulfilling, and our work of writing too, through the flow of coincidence. But only if we're willing to share our deep natures, our true selves.

As writers, this fulfillment can help us cope and thrive, as do the benefits of connection and meaning. Feeling satisfied with our life and our work is huge. Feeling complete in ourselves is too, and we will know what we want to say.

3: TYPES OF COINCIDENCE

Coincidence is clever. From an unlimited menu of selections it serves us our choices. From an endless array of possibilities it offers us what we want, in the form of meaningful events, choosing and blending the ingredients of chance, it seems, for our taste alone.

February, Keizer, OR: I began this new chapter on types of coincidence by writing these first lines. But then other things came up and I was drawn away. I decided to drive to a crafts store for diversion, and work later on. Before heading out I mentally asked to become aware of anything I needed to know about this section's subject.

Once at the store, I saw a special display. It was a sale on decorative papers, four sheets for a dollar. Several people were busily leafing through the stacks of assorted patterns for something that struck their fancy or their needs, and I started doing the same.

Let's back up a minute. I am not a craftsperson. I pretty much cannot *make* anything (okay, I did once come up with a couple decent-looking bookmarks through cut and paste) and it is not even fun to try. But I do love paper. So in addition to picking up vintage scraps of this and that, I sometimes buy colorful papers I cannot resist—to look at.

Back to our story: And then I found it. Prickles ran down my spine as I came across a paper—the paper I knew was for me. With its picture, and "thoughts of you" caption, there was no mistaking the meaning or message. I couldn't help smiling at the coincidence that was relevant to our writing and the workings of the Cosmos too.

This was what I saw.

It was an outdoor scene in coral, gold, and green, and a tall lacy tree with shade. In it sat a woman with a tree stump for a desk, and a laptop on it. She was a flapper gal, in vintage dress, with a blossom over one ear. Beside her sat a big stack of books. The lady from the past, it appeared, was busy at her writing in the present.

It took a minute to understand why the image spoke to me as it did, but then I saw it. What a clever example of my earlier written words! For the big U really does choose and blend the ingredients of chance for our tastes alone, mixing together in this instance a friendly caricature of me, the modern gal who loves vintage, and works on her computer, with books. Glad to have served as an example here of how this all works! Now on with our subject…

The two main types of meaningful coincidence are messages and materializations. These are the primary ways synchronicity operates and enters our lives. Within these types, however, will be an endless assortment of unique incidents. This makes perfect sense if you think about it. Our desires are for knowledge or circumstances. So the Universe answers through coincidental info, conditions, and things.

This spills over into our work in some advantageous ways. As writers, we use words to convey our messages. And the Universe will do the same for us. Answers about anything we want to know will often come through words. Because we're so aware of them, we're likely to notice and understand these meaningful coincidences. Even if some incidents feature other images or sounds, words may be a part of them too. So being good with words, as an author, has its perks.

Of course, any description of coincidence types is purely subjective, as the force can always create new ones. Or combine and rearrange elements of incidents at will. Still, here are some differences that are seen in coincidence, with a look at the varying words of each. Whether written, spoken, or a mixture of both, the big U speaks our language.

Solitary or Together

Some synchronicities concern just one. The answer given is for us alone. No other person is physically involved at all. In these instances, we happen across needed information via written or spoken words.

As writers, our messages often come through a myriad of written material—a note, a book, an ad, whatever—that we know is our answer. Others are involved as the source of the words, but not in the incidents themselves. We are the sole practitioner in these cases together with the Universe.

Like yesterday. I was feeling a little out of sorts. My writing was on hold due to some other obligations. Later, when I had time to work, I found myself pushing to try to get done what I hadn't before. And that didn't work. I couldn't *feel* my story, let alone write about it. So I quit trying, knowing I had temporarily lost my way.

I went online for a break to browse awhile and read a forum. There was a discussion going on about the creativity of writers. Authors were sharing their different approaches to working and the craft. It confirmed for me, coincidentally, what I already knew: we need to follow the flow of our own rhythm and pace, with how we feel as a guide. Then our writing will be what we want: heartfelt and meaningful.

With solitary syncs through spoken words, we are also the lone receiver. Others provide the info we need without knowing that they do. This may come through a friend, an acquaintance, or even a stranger.

We may talk to others about a subject of concern, or something different entirely. In either case, the answer to our needs comes through their comments. Or we may overhear a stranger's passing remarks, which may again offer the information we need, seemingly by chance.

Together, kinds of coincidence involve the needs of several people. A group may want the same thing, or each person something different. Either way, answers happen to come through something another person says. The incident plays out as questions somehow coincide and are separately answered.

For instance, maybe you're having lunch with a friend. It's fun and relaxing, and you're enjoying the meal. Still, in the back of your mind is a problem you're having finding time to write.

Your friend, it turns out, is having trouble sleeping. Though she doesn't say anything, it's also part of her thoughts, and has been for awhile, like your issue with time. So when someone sitting nearby says something about "choice" and "priorities" you each have a flash about that, which may lead to your solutions. All from someone who knew nothing about either one of you.

Major or Minor Role

Role assignment is a second common variable of synchronicity. In meaningful incidents we play different parts. As the recipient of our own coincidences we play the lead, while others support us. The Universe picks the perfect cast for its productions, even if some of them are unaware they're in it at all.

Answers may come through anyone involved in our

meaningful incidents. And alternately, through us in theirs. Everyone who plays a role, it appears, is essential.

Simple or Complex

Synchronicities can be plain and simple. They're easy to notice and easy to understand. Uncomplicated, pertinent responses to our needs and thoughts appear. They answer us clearly to help us write our best. Coincidental info or circumstances give us what we need to write with passion. When simple incidents occur we know we're in flow. It's all so easy! Feel, follow flow, write, repeat—plain and easy.

Maybe what we need is easy to arrange, Universally that is. Harmonizing the elements is simple and smooth. Or maybe in these cases, we are merely more alert, following the signs, doing our part. Talking to us then, about our work and our lives, will be easier. One thing's for sure: we've got to tune in. The simplest prompt can lead to much more, like this:

June, Keizer, OR: It was afternoon, and I'd gotten the urge to go over to the library. Keizer's tiny, volunteer-run library that is. So far, since moving here (Keizer adjoins Salem) I had never joined up. This sounds odd, I know, especially for a writer, and an avid reader too. But I used Salem's good-sized library, and was usually happy with their diversity and depth. Still, I was in the mood for a good mystery or two. And the tiny library was literally two minutes away. Plus I didn't feel like driving into Salem downtown with the extra traffic and all, so decided to stay close to home.

At the library I paid for a membership. There was no card catalog to search, but it was easy to see what was there. On a whim, I looked in the fiction shelves for one of my favorite authors, and found several of her books.

One I saw was unfamiliar to me. That was fun, for I'd already read many of her books several times each, and welcomed a brand new story. Oddly, this one wasn't at the Salem Library or part of its expanded network either. I was lucky, I thought, to have found it at all in such an easy way.

Turned out there was more than luck going on. The book ended up a good story, plus something more: the means to an answer about writing this book.

I was intrigued with this author's writing. She was popular a few decades ago with her novels of suspense. Each told a psychological tale that smoothly pulled you in; each was a mystery of mood and minds. More than anything, her sensual descriptions of surroundings were superb. Heroines found themselves in danger, in some strange places. And as you read of them you were right there too, experiencing all that she felt.

And that's what I aim for when writing: for readers to feel what I feel through the sharing of events. And that segues into the tense used for verbs in the writing itself. In my first book, I used present tense to tell the stories. So a coincidence description might begin like this: "It *is* morning, and I am eating breakfast out with Rae. We are talking about pie," as opposed to the more commonly used past tense: "It was morning, and I was eating breakfast out with Rae. We were talking about pie."

This worked well. The stories were open and observant and happening now, so the reader could be there too, feeling the full sense of the meaningful events. But there were problems when the incidents were told to me by others, as to which tense should be used, ending up with present for the telling, and past tense for their stories, like this:

It is morning, and I am eating breakfast out with Rae. We are talking about pie. Suddenly she leans forward in her chair and says with a grin, "Guess what Peekachoo (her dog) found last night? He was out by the back fence with his favorite toy. I called him over, and he trotted up with something in his mouth," etc., to the end of the coincidence story.

This also was effective to keep the stories real, but a bit tricky to write. I continually had to watch for slip-ups from the chosen tense. Still, I got through it, and the book turned out fine, and I was happy with the writing that let readers feel first-hand what I had as well. And I planned to work with incidents here in book two, just the same way. But that's not what happened.

I was working on this, about types of coincidence, and using the present for verb tense still, with the same question still circling in my mind. Could I write up the stories in past tense, yet keep them vibrant? It didn't seem so. How could stories of the past portray the feel fully now?

I decided to take a break and read an authors' forum for a while. When there I was surprised by a thread on this very thing! Writers discussing the use of present versus past tenses. I read the whole thing and came away with a simple solution to hopefully find my answer.

It was simple really. I'd take a look at the books of an author whose writing I liked and respected. Elementary, right? But I hadn't thought of it before, for whatever reason. See how she handled her scenes of description, through the tenses of her verbs. So I did, and was surprised to find past tense used throughout, which lessened none of the power of her words. It was an easy lesson, and felt right to do the same for this book.

Coincidences can be involved and complex, as well as simple, harder at times to notice and puzzling to read. They may answer us on more than one level, or in a deeper way, to help us with our work. Luckily we're not the ones who arrange their designs. With the help of the big U, complicated puzzles of words and events lead us to answers we need for our writing.

Incidents such as these amaze us with their complexity. Things leading up to them are intricately involved. For in our world, the coincidence must begin at an earlier time for its elements to come together so well. Take our last example. At what point did the events that resulted in the answer for my writing really begin? When I looked at my author's book for tenses? Found the thread on the forum? Became dissatisfied with the struggle of writing in present tense? Or did they begin earlier yet, when I first found the book at the library?

And what about others involved in the events, like the forum readers, for example? Had the originator of the thread I read just thought of the question herself? Or had the issue of tenses been one she'd considered a while? If so, the timing had to be right, to help both of us, while protecting our personal free will.

Whenever the process begins, there will be clues for us to follow, a path that leads where we want our writing to go— through coincidence.

Big or Small

Importance is another common variable of coincidence. Incidents vary from the big to the small. Some synchronicities are huge: messages relating to deeply meaningful aspects of our writing. Others are small: answers to questions about lighter things. Both are significant and will help our work.

It appears that the Universe treats all our questions with equal concern. Whether our thoughts are on something urgent, or something not so much, guidance will come as long as we've done our part by focusing on what we need.

It often seems that synchronicities about major matters are also complex, as if urgent, big stuff is hard to arrange, and that events about minor things are often simple instead. Though that may be so with mankind, it's not so with the Cosmos.

Sometimes the opposite is also true. When we're alert to

what's happening, simple signs may convey great insights or help for our writing.

The following cluster of incidents happened as I began this section. Their message for our work here finally made perfect sense to me.

May, Salem, OR: My friend Sophie and I had met downtown for coffee. As we made our way to a table, she touched my arm and said, "I can't wait to tell you about my miracle!" And as she had guessed, neither could I. So once we were seated she began her story before we talked about anything else—it was that important.

And fascinating. I watched her eyes shine as she shared her tale. But it was too private and personal and touching to even think of using here, and I knew it then. Yet later, I kept thinking of what she had said and the meaning of the thing, as there was a sense of something more. Something meant for me and my readers, as well as for Sophie, through her miracle.

A few days later I came upon a divination set for sale at a Goodwill store in Portland. This was unusual, as they rarely show up in any form at all. What was different about this set too was its theme of angels. Though I'm not a fan of the method, the book accompanying the angels divination deck looked interesting, to dip into anyway. So I bought the set, read a bit of the book, and re-donated it all, then forgot about the subject of angels. I thought.

A couple days later, I came across a charming little box, the color of cream. On its lid was a delicate raised design of an angel. I was delighted to find it, and oddly drawn to it as well, with no idea why. For really, I didn't know much about angels. But I wanted the little box, and liked how its pattern felt when I looked it. So I bought it for a few dollars, and took it home for a gift for someone or another.

Shortly thereafter, Eric and I stopped at a rummage sale in Dallas, near Salem. One room was full of holiday crafts. Underneath the tables were a couple dozen boxes overflowing with books. I made a beeline for them and started looking through them like a few other people.

Pretty quickly I came to an interesting-looking book—on angels. This wasn't surprising, as it was a sale being held by a church. But it turned out to be the only one on the subject it appeared, in the boxes. What drew me to it was its description, which spoke of miracles and coincidences; both Sophie's term and my own. I set the book aside.

Another browser noticed it, and asked if I wanted it. I said I did and asked, "Have you found anything good?"

She shook her head. "Not really. I'm just looking for one thing."

"What's that?" I asked.

"I am looking for books about angels."

Angels! There it was again, and this time from a stranger. I felt a tingle run down my spine. I wasn't sure what was up or what message there was for me, but I knew there was one. And I was anxious to take a look at the book—for whatever.

Later, I got a chance to do that, and was surprised once again. And it just took a moment to happen.

This is what happened. I didn't even open the book. It was sitting on the table next to me. I admired the golden cover and its lettering for the title, *A Book of Angels: Reflections on Angels Past and Present and True Stories of How They Touch Our Lives.* Then I consciously noted the author's name for the very first time: Sophy Burham. Once more that sense of tingly surprise. Sophy. Same first name as my friend of the miracle. And then I knew in a flash the meaning of the whole cluster of incidents.

The force is real. And it's there to help us write those things we are passionate about, that need to be shared. And it doesn't matter what we call it, or how we see it, or even if we totally understand it. So long as we are open to it, it's there. So what Sophie calls a miracle and I call a coincidence and someone else calls something else, is all the same. It's only our concepts that differ. And that doesn't matter to the Universe or the Force or whomever, as long as we do our part by asking, and being open to answers.

It seems strange at first that this even came up, with the theme of the book and all. Because that's what we've been considering—higher help for our writing. But the events were intriguing, the angels compelling, and their message insightful to me.

Oh, and there's a footnote. A month or so later I learned of a woman who had done a very kind thing. I told her she was a guardian angel. She liked that, and then I gave her the angel box that I just happened to have!

We also have many small incidents that benefit our writing, and are concerned with lighter things. They seem to arise and quickly conclude, if noticed. Some of these synchronicities are single events that provide what we're after; others are part of a group that does the same. Like always, the key seems to be to watch for them, and accept what they offer, whether big or small, one or several.

Let's take a closer look at those clusters.

Single or Cluster

Synchronicity varies by number. In regards to our writing, sometimes a single response from the Universe is all we need. Other times, it takes a cluster before we recognize the message, or understand its point. I know I can be pretty dense now and then, and clusters seem to happen at these times. It may be, too, that several incidents are needed to arrange things, even when we do understand.

Clusters may also be about several different aspects of the same thing. For instance, different aspects of one thing related to our work. When we're focused on our goal of writing with passion, the Cosmos is watching our back by providing guidance on the big picture. It seems that clusters of coincidences are sometimes needed to fully recognize or remember our own truth! My angels cluster was like that: a reminder of the importance of something I was taking for granted.

Literal or Symbolic

Synchronicities about our writing may be literal or symbolic. Answers may be based on actual wording, or something it represents. The same is true of other images or circumstances that are sometimes part of coincidence: they may speak in traditional or metaphoric ways. Though we'll look at these differences later, it's good to note them now. The language type in our events will be what suits us best.

The following event coincidentally conveyed a double message to me—unknowingly, through my husband. One part is about exploration on our writers' paths, and the second a sample of symbolic language for us here.

Eric had read something in the news that reminded him of this incident in the past, and he told me the story.

June, Central, OR: "It was summer, and I was solo backpacking in the Mt. Jefferson wilderness. The trail made a large C shape around two lakes a couple of hundred feet below. The terrain from the trail to the lakes was quite steep at the beginning of the C, but more gradual toward the end. Having come from the opposite direction earlier, I knew that my path to the trailhead was at the far end of the C.

"I was considering bushwhacking down to the lakes, as the terrain became less steep, even though you and I had agreed it was wise to stay on the trail when I was alone. When I reached the point where bushwhacking seemed most favorable, I came upon another solo hiker who was also considering the terrain. Turned out he had promised his wife that he would not bushwhack when by himself either.

"We talked, and realized that though our paths were different, they both took off from the lakes. He looked at me and said, 'Well, if we went down through this stuff together, neither of us would be soloing!' So that is what we did, heading down as a pair to the lakes, and then to our separate trails, both of us shortening our paths out, and getting a chance to bushwhack too. And without breaking our word to you, our wives!"

There was still a point about Eric's story I really didn't get. "But why did you want to bushwhack in the first place?" I asked. "Just as a shortcut?"

"That was only part of it. I'd been on the other trail several times before. This way was more adventuresome, offered a new perspective. I didn't want to lose my path, but I could still see the old one if I needed it."

4: SOURCES OF COINCIDENCE

As writers savvy of the secret of coincidence, we want to know its sources. Where do we find these mysterious messages? We really don't find coincidence. Rather, its signs and circumstances find us when we're focused. Then it's a matter of noticing them, and using them in our work. Though we've touched on some likely sources of events, let's explore a little more. Being aware of their origins will help us with our writing.

Visual Sources

Visual sources of synchronicity include words and images. Either can be single or multiple; i.e., one word or many; one image or several. Either can be public or personal; current or past, as well. Or a grand combination of these elements as best suits our needs. As writers, many of us are visually oriented, and naturally focused on words, for the reading and writing we like so well.

This segues into the prevalence of words that is often a part of coincidence. Words hold some pretty big advantages there. For starters, as our common symbols of language, we all know so many of them! And as the common way we think and know, words are great messengers—for the big U to help—to write to us.

July, Keizer, OR: I wrote my friend Amy in southern Oregon an email. We are long-time friends, and always stay in touch. Sometimes there are a few weeks in between our notes though. Anyway, Amy wrote back and told what she'd been up to, with gardening in particular, a favorite passion of hers. Then she added a footnote.

Amy said she'd gone to Smith River California for a couple of days. This is in the northwest corner of the state, on the edge of the redwoods. She said they'd stayed at such and such resort, which she liked very much, and that the weather on the beach had been pretty good. Reading this surprised the heck out of me, for just the day before, Eric and I had been online, planning a trip to that very spot, and considering the place where Amy stayed, to lodge ourselves besides!

What was odd was that I hadn't yet planned to start this section here today, consciously anyway. But an example for us occurred before I did. As in on some level it was known where I'd be heading. It's evident that arranging time is no big deal to the Universe, when speaking through written words, to help us share our topics with others.

As we would expect, written word coincidences occur through the writing of others, or even our own. They vary by time and place. Without being too technical, let's consider these common differences that might affect our work.

Public or Private

Sources of writing used by the Universe are varied and unlimited. Any recorded words may perfectly do. This information can be roughly divided into public or private writings. It's intriguing to imagine all the forms of public writing that might be used. Anything from ads to books to websites to so much more. What it gets down to is that anything written for a general audience might be used by the Universe, and noticed by us as writers. We pay attention to the words around us, after all.

Personal word sources are vast as well. Though not as visible as public sources, they are nonetheless there, in private locations or even secret writings meant for oneself or certain others. Letters, emails, notes to ourselves may all carry answers at some particular time—and provide it by coincidence.

Present or Past

Written sources may vary by time, as present or past writings. Our messages are via what works best at the moment. They also depend on what we like to read: current, older, or vintage books. As writers, we likely read literature from various eras, at different times, in an assortment of topics and stories. So paying attention to all of it is wise. Anything, written whenever, may hold a personal message to help us write with passion.

Let's stop a moment and remember an important point. We'll feel a draw. Certain words or images will pull, if they're meant for us. There will always be that feeling of something more in any synchronicity, even if it ends up being something small.

Our awesome synchronicities are exciting, of course, with their prominent events. But quiet insights, not so visible, can inspire us too. These may be subtle, yet lead us along, step by gentle step to personal truths that become a part of our writing. This often begins with words written in our favorite times.

This morning, home: I started thinking about the old letters again. These are the same papers mentioned earlier that played a part in some intriguing incidents told about in book one. I was fascinated by them then, and still am, and drawn to them then, and now, for whatever reason. Old paper has always been important to me, whether literature, notes, or scraps. There was a feel of ephemera that resonated with me. So I often satisfied my curiosity about people of another time by reading what they wrote.

A bit later, when I ran some errands, an ad on a van driving by offered "Lunch Box Delivery!" Immediately I envisioned lunch box socials, those old-fashioned romantic games of the early 1900s. Then my cache of old letters, again, whose authors may have played. I didn't know what the pull was, just that it was there, and had something to do with our topic at hand. So I decided to look at the letters again.

Later, I dug out the papers and made some coffee, and started reading the personal thoughts of those folks from the past, to learn from them a little more, and see what might be there. Quickly I zeroed in on one old letter that had fascinated me from the start, and still felt oddly like a message. About what, I was unsure, but I knew I needed to reread those old words again.

The letter was written by a gentleman in a tiny Kentucky town, to his family back home. He began:

(Town), Ky. Dec. 19, 1881

My Dear Son,

Your letter of the 16th with the $4 inside was recd. Next day eve—it came timely, for I had not a cent left and had to borrow, and owed my washer woman besides. Your proposal to send me money for current expenses is not objectionable except it might cripple your own finances— maybe it would be better to pay the groceryman a little along, to keep him in good humor.

Next month about Jan. 9th I can remit again, say about $70.00 or more, if I get my back pay. In the meantime, let Mother and sisters have what money you and (name) can spare to get them comfortable wraps for the cold weather. Don't let up on your effort to get Mother a good bench. I don't want her to take any more health risks at hard work.

Then he became playful, gently teasing his son about romance, and cleverly referencing a political idea and interest:

So the lasses 'O caught you with taffy hands stuck together. I expect if it had been your lips, they would have rendered assistance with greater gusto. Next time butter your hands a little—grease is a good thing, properly used— as politicians would say—as well as taffy.

My friend (name) was elected (position) unanimously. A week ago yesterday I took dinner at Dr. (name). They all seemed glad to see me. Mrs. (name) as usual had a good dinner.

Ending with some reassurances and sentiments for his family plus light humor about his own miserable situation:

Tell Mother I am getting along all right for health. Yesterday was a beautiful day, and (name), son of the (tailor?), loaned me his horse and saddle to ride to church at (town), about two miles away. I enjoyed the ride greatly. There was a good turnout. Everybody came on horseback or in buggies.

I would love to sit with you all, around our own hearth, Christmas Eve—away one day from the screams of noisy babies, the heavy tread of carpetless floors of Mash-men, Beer-runners, Hog-feeders, and Teamsters. But such is the part of the Store Keeper's life—what cannot be helped must be patiently endured...which I to my old, ratty wormy, weevilly, gloomy, dirty office go...

To Mother, Sons, and Daughters I send my love. Kind regards to neighbors and friends.

Your affectionate Pa, (name)

P.S. Instead of the Daily Commercial, send me the

Weekly—you can send it every week, send the back nos. in Dec. so that I can get all the Congressional news.

I finished the letter and felt its energy again, but not sure of what else. So I filed it in with some others and put them away. Yet the writer, and his heartfelt words, plus comment about patience, stayed with me, segueing into the similar idea of persistence, it felt, for us here. Persistence: perseverance, stick-to-it-ness. We all know the concept. And the value of having it, at times. But these times need to be when we are involved in working toward what we value.

There are always those other times too, when we stay with something we think we should, and gain nothing at all toward our heartfelt goals—what really matters to us. So those heartfelt goals are our key to it all.

Our Kentucky gentleman was a great example. Though we don't know a lot of details about his life, we do know a few, and a couple of what appear to be his passions. To begin with, he was an intelligent-sounding man. He wrote cleverly and insightfully about his thoughts and feelings. He used humor, wit, and gentle kidding to share with his family. And, of course, caring. More than anything perhaps, that caring for his wife, daughters, and sons comes through.

But that wasn't all. He seemed to have a keen interest in politics that went beyond a casual one, with three references to the subject in this one letter. Ending with a request to be sent the newspaper, he preferred to stay informed. His mention of a friend being elected to office concerned a major political role. So the feelings about the subject's importance seemed to be there.

We can sense his priorities of family and politics, played out in some pretty desolate surroundings. Mr. Kentucky was forced, it appears, to live temporarily away from home for some reason or another. He was scraping by—barely—by borrowing and "begging" for necessities, and by staying in a boardinghouse.

Even if we don't know what some of the boarders actually did for a living (I had to look up some of these colorful-sounding jobs!) we know they weren't the quietest guys to have around, along with noisy children as well. And we know Mr. K. was upset by that.

Then his office description, though written in jest, shows how miserable he was, some of the time anyway. Yet he concluded with a more positive remark about perseverance. Our gent seemed to have found a way for what he needed, and what he wanted to do.

Which brings up back to the point for our writing. We're going to have stuff happen that will challenge our goals, or maybe even our abilities to work at all. I know I do, and you will too. There will be times when people or events beyond our control interfere. We may have to stop writing for awhile—a few days or weeks, or whatever it takes in our situation.

But we can persevere. Like Mr. K, we can sit down to write about what we care about, when the babies are quiet and the lodgers have turned out the light. We can renew our writing when things calm back down. If we keep on trying in spite of stuff, we'll find our flow again back to deep feeling.

Written sources vary a lot depending on their age. Messages will arrive through words, old or new. Though current writing is familiar, older works may be used too, especially if we're attuned to their era.

Images are the other main visual source for coincidences. Like words, they may be public or personal, current or past. By images I mean any picture, figure, illustration, or object that we see, other than words. A single image is sometimes all that is used by the Universe as a sign. Other times a group of things are used instead. It seems that however we need to understand, that message is employed.

Combinations of words and images are common too. Our coincidences may include them both. In these instances, I think, all elements together speak better than one. It may be that we missed a simple answer, or didn't understand it, or maybe only partially so. In any event, an incident with both images and words occurs.

This can result in some clever combinations to help us with our writing. A huge source of images plus words for me is lost things I find tucked between the pages of books. As a fellow reader and writer, they may be for you too.

Forgotten Bookmarks

I don't know about you, but I don't always have a bookmark handy when I need one. No excuse for this really; it's not like I seldom read or something. Just the opposite. I buy books and borrow books continuously, and always have a couple piles of them I am reading, or planning to read next.

And besides that, I collect bookmarks. So have an assortment of them in the house, plus a few in my computer bag, etc. Still, there are times when I'm not near one of these, or whatever, and simply reach for something easy to mark my place, then manage to forget about it later. That's probably what happens to other people too.

What's most interesting about these is their variety. Items used to mark a page really only have one criterion: shape. Bookmarks work best if they're flat. So that explains the myriad types of paper pieces that are sometimes used, plus other flat things too, like ribbons, leaves, and flowers; pretty much any item that is naturally flat or can easily be pressed.

I have found a fun assortment of lost bookmarks through the years. At some point I started saving them—just storing them all together in a drawer really—so they'd be available because it was obvious right off that this was how the Universe sometimes spoke to me. I wanted to be able to keep them, and look at them, and enjoy their uniqueness too, because they sometimes held messages. And these needed to be remembered.

Of course, not every forgotten bookmark is a sign. Some of what we find is just that: something lost then found. But within our favorite spheres, words with images may be carrying info or answers for us. So it's wise to check the pages of any book that beckons, for treasures may be tucked inside; tiny treasures of rich insights on our writing.

My own collection of forgotten bookmarks is quite a mix. There are drawings, quotes, and clippings; tickets and cash. Pressed flowers, leaves, ribbons, and other non-paper stuff. Plus my favorite: readers' notes and lists. It's always a surprise to see what's been used to mark a page, and how that marker feels to me.

Are its words or images meaningful? Do they answer something I've been focusing on regarding my work? Do they inspire an idea I had almost forgotten about, like the bookmark itself? An idea pertaining to what I care about most? Sometimes a simple image and a few words via coincidence can do exactly that.

Like a few days ago. I had been at the library browsing for a novel or two to read. Right away I came across a couple of bookmarks. The first was a garden group's brochure that didn't interest me at all. The second was a temporary paper tattoo that did. Its image was of dolphins and a heart, and there were instructions for use.

This was something different than more common bookmark types, and I studied it a bit. Then its images quickly triggered some thoughts, of intellect (those smart dolphins) joined with feeling (that big heart) in our writing with passion, along with assurance of our freedom to change. For we can always shed the self we show the world and start over again, when and if we choose. And that was the message for me of the paper tattoo.

Interestingly the gardening theme of the other bookmark that seemed like nothing may have been something instead. I had taken it home anyway, and noted the theme. Then the next day, when taking a break from work, I found five more bookmarks, three also related to plants. I really took notice.

The entire thing was starting to feel surreal. While previously I had occasionally come across a forgotten marker, they now seemed to be everywhere, almost jumping out at me! So I saved these treasures too, their theme still a puzzle, and got back to our section here, and watched for the next piece to appear. That has only been a few days ago, and I'm still watching. I expect we may end up putting it all together later on, as the full meaning of their gardening theme becomes clear.

Many found objects besides bookmarks are image sources for me. Illustrations or figures may offer answers. Because I like shopping at secondhand stores, rummage sales and the like, the Universe talks through them to me, via pictures or designs. These messages usually include some words too, but not every time. An image may speak best alone. As always, the big U figures out the best language to use.

Advertising is another big image source for me. Its pictures and its words are often pertinent signs. In particular, I often receive coincidental messages through ads on cars and trucks. I really don't know why this happens, just that it does. Maybe because unusual or colorful ads have always been fun. It is one place I'm prone to look, that's for sure.

Images used for synchronicity also include patterns. Arrangements of repeated elements may speak to us. This is more likely if we are visual and like design. Decorations by man or nature include a palette of patterns, shapes, and colors. Any mixture may be used for meaningful messages that inspire us to write with feeling.

For instance, I have always been attracted to repetitive shapes in any form. Geometrics and florals are especially appealing. I love to study decoration on paper, objects, and architecture. In nature, the many shapes within moving water make me happy. I can watch the flowing colors and patterns of ocean waves or river rapids for hours, which sometimes results in insights or rousing for my writing as well.

How about you? Do you take in the world and learn mostly by what you see? Do you notice coincidences visually too? Knowing that in itself will be helpful to your work. Those of us who are visual will have synchronicities from sources we're likely to use: written words and images. What are your favorite types of these? Where do you see them most? Look to these areas to find your helpful answers.

Auditory Sources

Auditory sources of synchronicity include spoken words and other sounds. Both words and sounds may be public or private, and present or past. With these sources, clues arrive by coincidence through spoken words, music, or other noises.

Public or Private

Sources of speech and sound used by the big U are unlimited and diverse. Any spoken words or audible sounds may do. What that means is that anything spoken or played for a general or private audience might be used by the Universe, and offered to us as writers.

Think of entertainment, info and sales, and all that they entail, and their delivery via spoken words, plus music and the melodies of nature. And conversation, of course: what we say to others and what they say to us, perhaps the most common spoken words of all.

Conversations can share more than expected. Comments by

others may be just the info or answer we need. Sometimes we've asked and they know that, but other times they're not aware of anything at all. As writers we naturally notice words, and that's a good thing. The Universe may respond to our focus through the words of acquaintances, family, or friends.

I often receive information about my work via Eric. Many times this follows his bicycle rides. He meets the most interesting people along the way when stopping for breaks. Of course, he has no idea that something he repeats will be significant, ahead of time anyway. Just that the conversations he's had eventually are, and that I'm always eager to hear them.

Oftentimes a story by a stranger will be symbolic, meaning something different to me. Something related to writing with feel, along with serving Eric's needs, and that of the teller too, for socializing, rest, and all. I come away amazed each time this happens by the complex orchestration, and the helpful guidance I happen to receive.

Strangers may carry messages too. We may overhear a comment that answers some question, something we've been pondering. And that pertinent comment will come, it seems, right out of the blue. Or someone unknown will approach us to say a few words which do the same thing—coincidentally of course—and we're left with a feeling of awe about it all.

Cledons, these are sometimes called, messages by strangers. In ancient times some cultures had rituals to access this guidance. As writers we can remember how important eavesdropping once was, and watch for our own cledons. We can focus on our own questions, and then deliberately go out to listen. When we do, spoken words we happen to hear will often be meaningful.

Past or Present
Auditory synchronicities vary by time as well as by privacy.

Though most talk we hear is current, older speech is available too, through programs and other recordings of the past. Think of TV and radio of local or national news, politics and sports, music and all its lyrics. Any words from times gone by may coincidentally be used.

It's an incredible thing, the vastness of that pool with its depth of sources, including all ages and types of words. And if history is our thing—what we care and write about—we're likely to receive some answers through older spoken ones.

Music and Sounds

Coincidences may also occur through sounds other than words. Music and the melodies of nature can carry messages. These are often symbolic, as the arrangement and differences of tone serve as metaphors, reminding us of something more. If we're in tune to these songs, their lyrics will be bold and clear.

Melodies can help in another way too: by evoking that mind place where insights occur. As writers they'll be answers and intuitions about the spirit of our work, through the calling and coincidence of sound, and sometimes combined with sights as well.

Oceans always sing sweet songs to me, as I watch their dance of waves, inspiring and answering through both sight and sound. Time spent at the beach is soothing and special, and spills over into my writing, making it easy to flow from that deep space.

Deidre described reaching the same place through her piano:

"Playing music is kind of like meditation. I am not doing anything except the music. And after playing, I am usually very relaxed and content, so perhaps more receptive to clear thinking about something that's been on my mind. Also, I find playing to be satisfying, even if I'm struggling with the music. It just draws me into the experience, no matter what the experience."

5: UNDERSTANDING COINCIDENCE

One of the biggest challenges of writing in flow is understanding coincidence. We need to know what the curious incidents mean. Without this knowledge, the messages of personal signs will be lost to us, and no help for our writing. Fortunately, understanding synchronicities is usually not hard.

Our compass here is our feelings. As with every step in flow, something's sense is our guide. Following our energy leads to answers, or to the next step toward them on our path. What feels best and true for us is that.

This is not to say that understanding coincidence will always be simple. Some answers are much more complex. The depth of our questions, it seems, is the key. Simple questions will draw similar answers, while deep questions do the same, through many layered or complex ones.

Simple answers won't always be what we expect. We may hope for input about a plain question, and be surprised by what we get. This may be more information than imagined or something else related. What a boon this is for our writing! How great to be reminded of something important to include, some point unique to our work that we once knew, but have forgotten.

Like this morning. While driving through town, an ad caught

my eye. It was by one of those do-it-yourself carwashes, and read, "If in doubt, vacuum it out." What a strange sign! It took me a minute to figure out that they were encouraging people to clean their cars there whenever. But the "when in doubt" part of the rhyme threw me. Most of us don't fret over cleaning our cars or not, do we?

But because the wording was different and caught my attention (I seldom even noticed the business before) I considered it as a possible sign. Because when things stand out like this, we are often meant to see them. Then I mentally went over my focus of the last few days to see if there was a link, and this is what I found.

I'd been working on this section that you're reading. In fact, earlier that morning I'd written this part on surprises: surprising messages, that is, that remind us of something important to include in our writing. Then I saw the odd sign, with words that spoke of more to me than washing my car.

Understanding coincidence: when in doubt, wait it out. Start with a clear mind about what we think a sign might mean. This message surprised me. The start-with-a-clean-slate aspect of it was simple once I thought about it, symbolized by the "vacuum it out" part of the ad. But that I had received it right then was unexpected.

And, as always, that was helpful, for I hadn't made notes in my outline about the idea at all. Not that I hadn't ever thought of it, because I had, and practiced the concept at different times. But I hadn't remembered to include it here and was being reminded to do so.

So when in doubt about a message, wait it out instead of guessing. There's likely to be more to come. And the answer that we get may be nothing we expect, and in many ways more helpful. Sometimes we will end up waiting quite a while for our answers, as though we are not quite ready for what the Universe wants to say. So instead of spontaneous knowing, we come to understand a sign days, weeks, or even months later. An instance of that may be happening right now, coincidentally, as I write these words, and concerns an unusual conversation of this morning.

I was talking casually with someone I'd just met about impersonal things. We spoke of children, and he said he had a young daughter, and that he and his wife had another on the way. Then he shared something highly unexpected and unusual: that when he looked into his daughter's eyes, it was like an old soul was looking back.

And that the girl wanted the new baby named Lucia, and also had a toy cat she'd named Burma! He had no idea where the child might have heard these names, or if she ever did. But he knew his daughter was smart and unusual. By the sound of it I agreed and knew I'd love to meet her.

Later I thought about the oddity of the man even telling me this. We had just met, after all, and knew nothing of each other. Yet a few minutes into our talk this fascinating disclosure began. It gave me goose-bumps at the time, with questions right after. And was there more to it, as in a message for me? What was going on with this girl and her attraction to a name from the past? It was eerily different, of that I'm sure, but nothing more yet. But I will write it down in the journal and here—and in time we will see.

Sometimes a synchronicity takes some steps before we know what it means. This can be fun and fascinating. In these cases, each step takes us a little deeper into some kind of understanding that maybe one sign couldn't do, or maybe that we missed, or just didn't get the first time around.

The following stirred some insights on the nature of deep writing through feelings fountain-penned a hundred years ago.

August, Keizer, OR: It was early morning. An image from a dream woke me right up. Which was a shame, because at some level of that deep sleep mind, I knew it was an extra meaningful symbol. So I laid there thinking about it, and tried to remember more about the special book in the dream.

This was no ordinary book, but an antique Victorian autograph book instead. Its cover was rich wine velvet, with ornamental gilt letters spelling "ALBUM" on top. The pages were cream, filled with fanciful sepia script of that earlier time. And as I watched, someone or something was opening those pages.

I knew they were being opened for me. There was a message within the entries of that book I was meant to read. But just as that certain page appeared and the copperplate writing cleared, I woke up. What a disappointment! It felt like a treasure hunt with vanishing clues that were meant to mark the trail after already glimpsing the prize at the end.

I decided to try to reenter the dream by going back to sleep. But that didn't work at all. So I ended up getting up, and on with my day, with the essence of that old book on the edge of my mind. So I decided to honor that, and pursue it, to see where it might lead through a literal treasure hunt.

An antiques mall downtown was my first destination. I hoped to find an album similar to the one in the dream. I didn't know what that might prove. But I did know that I felt the urge to look further, to follow the dream's energy—to wherever.

I didn't find anything in the mall. No albums or diaries or journals from earlier times. And then in a second store that said yes, we get them, check back, there was nothing either. Later when I looked online, there were dozens available. But buying one there didn't feel right at all. I wanted to hold the book and read some of its entries to know if it spoke to me. So I decided to do nothing—simply wait—to see what would happen next, if there was a message I needed to hear.

The following day a neighbor came over. He'd gone to the state fair and noticed some local authors set up with their books. He said that he's like an autographed book of mine. The similar wording to what I'd been looking for felt eerie, and tickled me besides. We'd been living near each other for a year, but right then was he interested. The coincidence was too right on, and clarified the meaning for me of the symbol.

The autograph. Our signature. The personal way we choose to write our name in letters. Also that act of writing by hand. The autograph book. An album full of signatures as well as best wishes by their authors. The Victorian album. A book of bittersweet good wishes, sentimental memories, and sometimes trite rhymes as well.

It's really no surprise that the old book made it into my dream. I respect the Victorians' loyalties and caring natures. The album with conflicting contents of deeply felt sentiments or shallow clichés may have symbolized our writing. So in the books we write, our passions must come through our personal voice and our words. For every book we write is really an autographed one.

Dreams: imaginations, reveries, night-time visions; stories of inner symbols and signs. Our dreams may be linked to meaningful coincidence. Dreams as in an inner state like insights and thoughts may be linked to outer events, and may play a role in their appearance.

It seems the Universe must use various props to get our attention. And sometimes several, not one. So inner signs such as intuitions and dreams may be coupled with coincidence. Yet sometimes the former are enough by themselves to deliver a message.

When I first started writing for the Internet, I couldn't find a place to work—a place I was happy with anyway. After traditional jobs, working at home felt too quiet and lonely. But alternately, though cafes were busy with people, they were often too loud. Outside spots weren't right either. Weather and temperatures were too iffy for more than occasional sessions.

Then I had a dream. In it I was carrying my laptop from place to place, trying to write. One spot was too quiet and the next too loud until I found—a library. How simple was that! And there the surroundings were right what I needed.

When I awoke I felt kind of dense. And I couldn't figure why I hadn't thought of working there before. Especially since I spent a lot of time browsing the books already. But the dream pointed out clearly and literally what I seemed to be missing.

Sometimes it's different. Our dreams may offer help in a symbolic form, or portray events that coincidence repeats. In these instances, it seems the big U knows we need a couple kinds of nudges to pay attention to its answers.

The following cluster shows how mysterious dreams can be, and how meaningful for our writing. And we don't have to understand just how they work to benefit from their signs.

Deidre told me the first story right after my own album dream.

September, Corrales, NM: "I went down to Sara's with the intention of just going around with her for some errands, and then to the growers' market. Well, we ended up at this cute little boutique, and I found a wonderful outfit that EXACTLY fits Deidre! When I got home and showed Adam my purchases, he told me that last night he'd had a dream about a conversation with me where he said, 'Why don't you go shopping and find some new clothes?' Weird. Did I somehow hear his dream?"

I wrote back telling her about researchers I'd read about who teach shared dream work, where several people are said to experience (and literally visit!) the same dream world. She answered, "Shared dreams, hmm. I've been thinking about this. It is weird because I don't recall dreaming anything about this at all, but later Adam told me about his dream, and it fit perfectly with the real event. Another interesting point was that it was Sara's idea to stop in and look in the little shop Voila!"

She went on, "I love these o-d-d experiences. I can't help but think I was party to Adam's dream. Just feels right to think that anyway. All I know is that when Sara and I walked into this little shop, I loved the first thing I saw (a jacket), and it was the only one left, in my size. And the pants I bought were the only ones left in that style. It was like I was meant to have this outfit. This is not the kind of shopping I ever do, but I was so happy when we went home. The Universe was extra kind to me today!"

I came away from her story as I always do with these tales, feeling pretty grateful. How lucky to be able to learn about these things! But just as much fun is that magic we experience through our own coincidence. So what it came down to was confusion. I felt certain Deidre's incident was also meant for me and our writing with passion work here. But I hadn't an inkling how.

Watching for clarification usually works well for puzzling events like these. We can mentally ask our questions and focus on that, then be aware for any pertinent signs that might arise. But I was extra curious, and hoped to learn something right then.

In particular, should the topic of dreams be included more than briefly in this book? They were coming to my attention more often for sure. And I wanted to adapt my direction if that was the case. And what did Deidre's coincidence mean for us here? Becoming clear on these points was surely my next step.

I decided to consult the tarot. I felt like doing so was strange in itself with my beliefs about it, for I'd come to find that we're always the best interpreter of guidance, that the meanings of messages we come up with ourselves are usually right on, much more than the fixed ones of any type of divination. Still, these systems can trigger our knowing, and I was eager for that, and felt a nudge toward the cards.

Following my vibes, I dug out the deck and shuffled the cards a while. Then, while thinking of my question—is it important to explore dreams more in the book?—I drew one. A major arcane card, The Star, is what I picked.

Stars: celestial twinkling lights linked to guidance and good luck; shimmery points that show the way. Heavenly signs of beauty by the Divine, for ancients.

So stars have often been symbols of links to Spirit as well as shining guides, with magic associations too.

The card's connection with dreams felt simple. Like stars, dreams appear in the night to illuminate our way. They light up our true feelings, and clarify our path. They offer wisdom and answers and wit. From a creative force in the night like the stars in the sky, they're there.

I didn't know if the symbolism was the same in tarot, so I looked up some meanings from different kinds of decks. There were a few variables, but guidance and light were key, plus symbolizing the sight to be able to see signs. And right there it all clicked: my recent dream-time book, plus my thoughts about Deidre's story. And I understood the answer was yes, talk more about dreams; share a few of your own special ones, for dreams play a role in coincidence at times.

One of the earliest life-changing dreams I remember involved focus versus freedom. I'm not sure when I dreamt it, which was some years ago, but I knew it was special when I did. Its message was powerful, and has helped me reach my aims ever since it happened. It also pertains to how we want to write, so may be of help here.

The setting was some kind of gym. I was standing, along with a few others, next to a floor mat lying under a rope. The rope was thick and heavy and suspended from the ceiling. There was a speaker; a clear invisible voice, keeping track of what was going on. I watched someone swing out on the rope a few times and then it was handed to me.

My style was different. I swung first in one direction and then another, in a random manner. But I couldn't get going very well at all. There was no power there to propel me where I wanted to go. Then the voice said, "If you swing in one direction you will go farther." Immediately I tried that, and sure enough, my reach was much better than before. Then, feeling a little doubtful, I thought to myself, but what if I want to *change* directions? Instantly that then happened, and I swung strongly in another straight line, as far out as the rope could reach.

That focus versus freedom theme had long been with me. I'd always wanted the freedom to explore new things. And the idea of focusing on something single seemed, well, counteractive to that. But often I had headed in so many directions that I didn't get anywhere at all, and that was what the dream was all about.

I've gotten better. The dream was an eye-opener into blocks I was building in front of my personal goals. By refusing to choose, I was really limiting and not keeping my freedoms, for I was not staying with anything long enough to find out if I liked it or not.

So flexibility that allows us to explore depends on some structure. There's energy behind that focus that we can always choose to change. And that energy is needed when we want to write with passion. Our outline's the form we can follow as planned, or detour and later rejoin based on the insights and inspirations of meaningful coincidence.

A second personally big dream that I mentioned before was about coincidence, and the power of focus, again. It feels worthwhile now to share its details. The dream took place on a college campus that was colorfully lush, with flowers and grass and trees everywhere. I was busy trying to reach some place or other, but having trouble doing so, for all the surroundings like buildings, and benches, and those tall, tall trees kept changing! I wasn't a bit happy about that, and complained aloud. Then I was taking to a big book of "Explanations." (I know; yet another book.)

The book fell open to a ribbon marked place. There, the left page was titled "Permanent Reality," and the right, "Flexible Reality." I was shown through moving pictures how reality changed based on the thoughts and beliefs we held. To reach any goal we had to concentrate on it. Then, a path to that place would appear among those changing elements. And there would be signposts to guide us, as long as we stayed focused.

And there we have it once more: the importance of continually choosing our goals in our lives and our work. With our writing, it's helpful to know our focus every time we start to write. This may be a mood, a scene, a topic; whatever we want to convey. Then, with that aim in place, our route will stay clear, often through ongoing clues.

A third helpful big dream was on something far different: the importance of humor to our work. Here's what went on in this strange night-time scene. It was afternoon, in a spacious, grassy park. The sky was deep blue overhead on that luminous, sun-lit day. I was lying on a small, green hill, enjoying the cotton clouds above. Then, in the middle of my play—splat— something fell onto my face.

Startled, I jumped up and looked all around. Seeing nothing unusual, I laughed at the joke. For it felt obvious that someone was jesting and playfully kidding me, though someone or something that I couldn't see.

Then I took a look at what had fallen down from the sky. It was a gorgeous golden fragrant rose with no stem. How impressive! But where did it come from, I started to wonder, and how was it able…oh, it was just some kind of fluke, I thought to myself. Then, sensing the wrongness of that, I thought again.

No, it wasn't that: it was a gift; a sign from above. And right there the dream ended.

Later, I considered the message of the dream. I thought of my mixed feelings for roses (love their fragrance and flowers, their foliage not so much). It seemed clear that the big U was both generous and light-hearted with its gifts to us, plus knew just what we liked. It was the dream's humor though that felt most important to me when I reflected back upon it.

We all know how much enjoyment humor can add to our lives. Seeing the funny side of things is just plain fun. More than that though, being able to laugh about things helps us not take ourselves and our work too seriously. When we write about what matters in a lighthearted way, our theme will be comfortably clear, instead of feeling heavy or forced. Being sincere about our passions is helped, not hindered by humor!

Maybe hearing about a few of my big dreams has reminded you of your own dreams that had to do with your writing. For when we share deeply through our words, they are apt to surface there. Our dreams may offer guidance on their own or with coincidence, so keep track of your big ones.

A good place to do this is in a journal. Though we'll talk later about recording research and ideas, personal journals work well for dreams. These can be separate books or combination coincidence ones. I try to record all my coincidences, plus those that I'm told by others, and a few special dreams. And I like to do this by hand. Decorative journals are my favorite books for this. It's fun to search for a new book when the old one is full, with just the right look and feel.

Because journals are so popular, there's a wide variety of colors, designs, and sizes available. Quotes and sayings on covers or pages are an option too. I am partial to these in particular. It's fun to find one with thoughts on ideas, creativity, and writing that speak to us. And that may inspire our own flow of words. For these reasons, I collect small journals, and always have a few stacks of them around. It's enjoyable to look at them and read their sayings, even if they're empty for awhile.

Recording our incidents helps us understand them, whether immediately or later. We can look back to review what happened. This in itself can trigger new insights and realizations about them. As some meanings of coincidence unfold over time, it's really the easiest way to be sure to understand them when they do.

Recording synchronicities can be brief or detailed. Depending on other things, this often will vary. What's most important is writing down our incidents however feels best at the time. It works well to add the date and location, plus a few key words for a title that tell what the event was mostly about. That's really all we need to put down. We can experiment with this, trying out different formats in our journals if we like. I'll share more on my own journal structure later on.

So once we've experienced a coincidence, we'll want to understand its meaning; what its personal message is for us. This may be easy—we'll just know right away—or it may take time, needing more thought or clues. Before we can benefit from answers though, there's one more step to do, and that is simply to respond.

Our responses may be easy, following up with action that is almost automatic. Answers come quickly through coincidence with just what we need. Our response is quick too, once we have that info or green light signal.

Like this morning, Eric brought up an herbal tea that he was curious about, and that he didn't know I had thought about the day before. Then a few minutes later, he opened a newspaper section to an ad and coupon for the same product. It felt like a go-ahead to us, and we made a note to look into the tea; our easy response.

Sometimes it's that simple with our writing too. Our work-related need is quickly answered and we respond in kind, hardly needing to think. We know what we need to do next, and do that. The Universe offers help through coincidence, and we follow up from there.

Other times it's not so simple. There are events we feel are messages, but we don't know what they mean, nor what is next for us to do. But if we stop a bit and wait, without pushing on, things are likely to become more clear through additional prompts and clues that will lead toward our writing goals.

We can also refocus; go over our question, mentally ask what we need to know, or refocus on our goal, where we are aiming, if we know our intention. These two responses, patience and re-asking, should get things moving again, and help us read the meaningful messages that come when we do.

PART II

6: INSPIRATION

Where do we find our stimulus and ideas to write with passion? Almost anywhere. The world is a curious and inspiring place. When we are focused on what we care about, and attentive to our surroundings, the insights will come—and oftentimes through coincidence.

One mind frame seems essential. We need to be relaxed and at ease. Only when we are do we notice intuitions and signs. And it seems that both these kinds of messages, the inner and outer ones, play a part in inspiring us to write what we feel.

A second state of mind, openness, seems essential as well. We need to be willing to receive. When we're open to different possibilities, the Universe answers. This is not to say that being receptive changes our minds about things, but that it may rouse it instead, to discovering our own special truth. And sharing that truth is what our writing is all about.

So what are good sources of ideas? What places or activities can inspire us? Once we're focused on our topic, relaxed, and receptive, what can we do? A few pastimes in particular will help us tap into our muse.

Travel is at the top of my list of inspirational sources. And by travel, I simply mean moving from one new place to another. So a day spent poking around a nearby park can be as beneficial, writing-wise, as a month-long excursion. "Newness" is the key word here, even if it only describes a spot that's just a little unfamiliar, or has changed a little bit since you last were there. Newness for our purposes is special.

Newness in any form can inspire us. Thinking, feeling, and acting in unfamiliar ways can stimulate ideas. It seems that doing things differently lets us see things clearly, that we couldn't see before. With the additional guidance of the Universe, of course.

Travel is one of the best sources of this. When we take any kind of trip, the new sights we see and sounds we hear affect us. We may participate in activities that also are new. Interactions with others while traveling can provide new perspectives on most anything at all. Just going someplace different and experiencing what's there can help us know what's best for our lives.

April, Salem, OR: While I was planning this chapter of the book, I received confirmation of the importance of including travel via Eric. Just home from a bike ride, he entertained me with this story:

"Next to a little store near Brooks, I came across a bicyclist having coffee. I bought myself a cup and we started talking. Since he was loaded with touring gear, I asked about that; where did he start from and where was he going? A cross-country trip was the answer, from one corner of the US to the other!

"Then he told me about an extraordinary trip of some years before. Due to a mid-life crisis, he had ridden around the world! I was blown away by this—the guy had ridden thousands of miles through dozens and dozens of countries. I really enjoyed his story, and talking with him made me think about possible rides of my own."

So here is the repetition of the idea of the inspiration of travel.

Eric happens to bump into a guy who has used it to expand his thoughts. His take in itself was inspiring, and we hoped the trip worked out for him—and it probably did—as he was busy riding toward the horizon again.

This theme of mental outlook and travel was repeated once again a day later. After lunch at a Chinese food restaurant, I broke open a fortune cookie to find, "Travels away from the next will broaden cultural horizons."

Yes! The meaning of the message hit me at once. I was being reminded a second time of the importance of including the material in this book. But hadn't I already done that, in my notes anyway? It felt like there was more to come on it somehow. I had no idea what that might be, but would be watching.

How do you like to travel? By taking short day-trips to check out new places? Or longer excursions with plenty of time to explore? Do you like to plan the details of what you'll see and do, or wander more at will? Whatever your style, experiences on trips can inspire your writing. So take along a journal to record those prompts.

A second inspirational source for our writing is recreation. During enjoyment, insights can occur. This probably works as well as it does because we're apt to be receptive when we play. And so if gardens are fun for us, for example, or garage sales, or carpentry, or whatever, there's a good chance we're relaxed when we enjoy them, yet also alert. And that makes us open to signs.

It doesn't really matter what recreation we do. As long as it's amusing to us we'll profit with inner and outer messages that pertain to our writing with feel. Sometimes these are comprised of simple insights that help us know our truth, and triggered by the activity itself.

For instance, I've read a few books by ardent knitters on the nature of their craft. These books were not about technique as much as zeal. The artists had discovered parallels between knitting and truths of life, from their passionate point of view.

Others learn from music or mechanics or a myriad of different things that proved to be insightful. Their activity itself provided the clues. Materials, tools, or steps they took were the stimulus. But sometimes sights or sounds nearby can inspire ideas too, when we're doing something enjoyable. That was the way for me, when envisaging this book.

January, Keizer, OR: I was shopping in an import store, one of my favorite activities. I really love exploring their assortment of fun, unusual wares. Percolating in the back of my mind was the question: what should be the theme of my next book?

I knew that since coincidence was my thing, it would be about that. And about writing too. More than anything I loved to research and share about them both. And often incidents occurred, coincidentally, that helped me write about the same, while I was involved in doing just that! So I wanted to combine these two topics: coincidence and writing in my theme. But I didn't exactly know how. That's what was in my mind as I began to browse.

Pretty quickly I came upon a display that grabbed my attention. It was a collection of monogram mugs with initials on the front. Though each one was lettered, it was different too, through its colors and floral designs. The cups were charming and bright and they reminded me of something or other. I looked at them again and then the answer was right there. They reminded me of writers!

Each of is like the mug with its initial in common with some others. But each has a special background design as well. It's this uniqueness—our special way of understanding things—that we must write about, to enliven the truth of our words. It's great that we're encouraged, when we focus on that truth, through coincidental signs. And some encouragement of my own was delivered right then.

May, Keizer, OR: I had written about two types of sources here, and there were a couple more I planned to do. Inspiration for our writing really could be found anywhere! Though there are no set categories, I hoped I was highlighting enough possible ones to show that this was true.

Later, I was at the mall, again in the import store. There was a fine display up front of journal papers and pens. One book with the image of an old-fashioned typewriter on the cover, and a thought about "ideas," looked especially fun.

I looked inside the book. On the first page was a quote about the prevalence of inspiration! Another quote later on listed possible sources too. I looked them over, and realized in a flash that I was being encouraged to expand my ideas about sources here, for more understanding. Naturally I also bought the journal, that seemed made just for me, to keep track of messages of my own.

Exploration is a third great source of inspiration for our writing. When we're curious, ideas abound. So as long as we're relaxed and open, coincidences about our work are apt to occur. By "curious," I mean eager to learn about what attracts us, inquisitive to check into what makes us feel. Even if we don't know *what* we feel, that we feel is itself enough. When we're willing to investigate, in time we will.

Anything we explore can inspire us. We may be drawn to certain images, sounds, or things. Particular places and forms made by nature and man may speak to our spirit. When we're curious and follow these clues, we end up where we need to be for receiving ideas. I was led to such a place by a playing card, while writing my first book on coincidence.

It began with an ace of spades card found laying in the road. It felt strange this time to see it—as there had often been images of the same—and I felt curious why. So I set out to study the symbol and see what then.

What happened was astounding. I was led along a path of coincidences all involving the ace, and all providing messages on writing and life. Being curious, it seems, is crucial to what we want overall. To write about what we care about with passion! (And yes, the whole detailed story is in the other book, in case you'd like to share it.)

Another time a cache of old letters held the key. I became curious after finding them in a shop, so I bought the whole bunch, and began a weird exploration of people from the past, and ended up with connections and inspirations for my subject and my writing—by coincidence. (This one's in there too!)

When we're eager to know about things we see, or hear, or do, and feel something too, it behooves us to explore. What are you curious about? You might happen upon some rousing ideas by checking them out.

April, Salem, OR: Our cousin Trudy was visiting from out of state, and we were at the library. She's an avid historian, her passion is genealogy, and she shares her findings with others. She also writes true stories about her ancestors for the family. Right then Trudy was looking for books that showed early Norwegian borders, to figure out where some people were born. But she hadn't found any in the stacks, which was disappointing.

Then we learned that a book sale was going on downstairs. It was a semi-annual event to benefit the library. Trudy checked it out and found a couple of books with the information she needed seemingly by chance. We agreed that the library sprite was busy sprinkling stardust around.

Reading is a source of inspiration we probably take for granted. As writers, especially, we often turn to books. Many of us love to read for amusement and for pleasure; it's a fun and favorite part of what we do. So when we strive to write our best—with deep feeling and truth—it's natural that we turn to books as well.

There are a couple of approaches we can take to our reading: traditional research or to go-with-the-flow. The second approach often works best for our aims and desires here. We can base the reading and research we do for our writing on intuitions and signs.

I am pretty much always looking for books. By that I don't mean some kind of rigid plan. What I mean is that books are so magical and surprising that I'm always on the lookout for good ones. And when I find them, I need to read them if it feels there's maybe something there for me.

Your especially good ones will be different than everyone else's, and personally attuned. How you find them may be ordinary or not. Though we often find our books in the usual places—bookstores, libraries, etc.—sometimes we don't, but in unlikely spots instead, by coincidence.

Think about secondhand sources. The old saying about one person's treasure being another's trash is often true. This brings to mind thrift stores and antique shops. Also garage sales and estate sales too. Basically any place of recycled or discarded things.

A perfect example of this happened a year or so ago in our family.

Eric's cousin Trudy needed to sell a library when her sister died. Some books were about Russia, and some written in its language. She advertised the collection, but got no response at all. Then something uncanny occurred. Trudy's sister Suzanne appeared in a dream with a message. "Don't worry about the books," she said. "The problem's been solved!"

Shortly thereafter a woman called about the collection. She had heard about it from a friend, and was very happy at that. Turned out she had been looking for Russian books to teach her kids at home, and hadn't found what she needed until then. Talk about a strange win-win coincidence!

Though I haven't found many books outdoors (no, I do not do garbage cans), I have found items in campgrounds, parks, and such: things lost by others and found by me. And these can be books. So the best thing for us writers is to aim to be aware, wherever we are. Books that inspire us can show up most anywhere. Like this:

Today, Salem, OR: I was getting ready to run some errands. I was also thinking about coincidence and inspiration for writing. Mentally I asked to be reminded of any important points I may have forgotten for the book, and decided to consider anything unusual I came across as a possible sign.

Later, after finishing my errands, I stopped in at the Goodwill. The store was busy and full of shoppers. Wandering around, checking out this and that, I wound up in glassware. There was an impressive assortment of dishes of various types. Tucked in amid a display of mugs and cups I spotted something odd and clearly out of place: a box with the word "oracle" on the side. (I don't know why I often find strange stuff mixed in with the cups of these places; I just do!)

I pulled it down from the shelf to get a closer look, and found that it was a divination set of Asian design. There were bamboo sticks with painted tips, and a tiny hardback book, containing history of the system. Plus "answers" and an exploration of how it all works.

It didn't take an oracle or wise one for me to know that this was my sign. I could intuitively feel its pull, plus it was an unusual thing to find. In all my years of thrift store shopping I had never come across something similar. Not that it was rare or anything; it was just an inexpensive little set. But finding it there was not the norm.

But what was the message for me? To include a section on divination in the book? That is plausible, as both synchronicity and divination communicate through meaningful coincidence. But I don't much care for the fixed interpretations of these systems. Yet the set and its purpose were pertinent to what we were doing here. And I felt there was something more. So I bought it and brought it home, to think about and share.

Once there I pulled out the dictionary, though acquainted with the word I wanted to find. "Divination," I read, then one of its meanings: a telling by inspiration. Inspiration? That was surprising listed there. But then, there was the link, for I was in the middle of writing about the same. Maybe that was what this was about: another inspiring source, to help us with our writing? I needed to read the little book that came with the oracle set.

When I did, I found that it answered through symbols. Qualities of nature were used to explain. After asking a question, a person was led to a symbol to read about its traits. This description is then pondered and considered a response.

As with all divination, intuition is used to look for connections. The symbol answer is read and explored. If it offers insights about the person's need or desire, the inquiry is a success. But what about imagination? Can't anything, really, be linked with another thing through that? Not really. Here is why this is so.

It's a stretch. It is not a good fit, and we can *feel* the truth of that if we try. So if we have a concern we are focusing on— something, for example, like: why don't I stick to my exercise plan?—and choose any old thing to find an answer, it just doesn't work. And any answer we come up with feels forced, and we know it.

In our example, say we see a vase on the table and try to use that. We note its rose design, then work to link it somehow to our question about exercising. So we might grapple with it like this: I don't keep up my exercise plan because…the air is not as sweet as in the summer? No, that's not it. Because…I don't want to be seen walking unless I look as fresh as a rose? Nope, hardly! That's not a concern at all. Etcetera, etcetera. It just doesn't work.

Alternately, divination may lead us to our answer through a random symbol we happen to choose. And if it does we'll feel the rightness of the message. Still, more steps are needed to get there though, through all the fixed meanings, to that answer that's personally right and true. Much easier I think to let the big U choose our symbols.

The books that go along with divination sets can inspire us though. Even if we don't use the systems, their suggested answers make us think, and recognize our own truth to tell. The methods deal with life, and what's most important there, just like our writing. So that may serve as a source for us as well. We can read the literature with no set plan, if that feels right to do.

Research

Selective reading of the books of others will be part of our work. Research can inspire us. How we research, though, may be different than most. As we strive to write with feeling by following flow, we're likely to research the same way: by noticing energy and signs.

It works well to make tentative research plans as with other steps of our writing, like a list of the books we know we want to read. This gives us a place to start our study of other works, and a sense of direction too. But with the big U involved, it's only a sense.

Here's what is likely to happen. As we read the thoughts of

others, new ones will occur, from our personal perspective of truth. We'll have urges to follow threads of ideas we never knew before. If we do, branch off and look into something else that calls; we're apt to end up curious and inspired.

We can keep following these threads which may lead to new insights, and add to our writing with interest and depth. And if they don't, we can make notes of what we find for future reference. Ideas can come together in surprising ways at unexpected times. The important thing is to capture our thoughts along with a few good notes.

I take notes of anything that speaks to me. When I read books related to my topics or those that aren't, I write down these parts. This might be a few words, a phrase, or even a paragraph or two—whatever appeals. Then occasionally, while writing, I read these over, allowing my own insights to emerge.

The ideas of other writers should remain just that, their own ideas, but they may still be helpful to us. A good way to look at their work is as a catalyst only, to inspire our personal voice. And that's what our writing will be made up of, our personal passionate views; the ones we want and need to share with readers. So it works well to record special bits from the books of others; any thoughts or info that makes us feel.

I take all my notes by hand. This goes along with some other steps I choose to do that way. You may like technology better, taking notes on your favored device. We'll be talking here about the first method. Adapt as you wish.

Hardback notebooks work well for research. They are for sale with office supplies. I buy mine in several colors at a local stationery store. They come in different sizes too, so choose what seems best. You can always choose again if that doesn't work out.

Note full particulars about each of your sources. If you end up quoting or referring to anything from a book or other publication, you'll need them for your book's References section. I refer to very little of other authors' material. When I do, I fully cite the source, and request permission first from both the author and the publisher. Play it safe and do the same.

In the margins of your pages, list a few words about the subject of each section. This is an easy way to organize your notes. If at a particular point you want to see what you have on a particular topic, it is not hard to scan these labels.

You can make an index of these topics too, though it's not necessary. If you end up with a lot of research material, a hard copy or computer doc index will help you locate things faster. You might consider transferring all your reference notes to a document file at that point too, if that feels right to you.

Coincidence Journals

Let's explore journals in more detail here. Notebooks are valuable to writers, especially on the go. And for those who write with passion, they're particularly so. I sure didn't set out to make these two sentences rhyme, but maybe it's good they do. Their rhythm may help us remember the idea. As writers on the lookout for inspiration, we need our journals!

By journals, I simply mean a place to capture our coincidences and our ideas. These can be combined or separated as you choose. I usually record all synchronicities I experience in one journal, and everything else in another. This works well, but as long as you know where to find what you're after, either arrangement will do.

Since meaningful coincidences are the tool many of us have been missing in our work, we want to capture every one. They will help us write our best, with passion. Though we won't always understand them right away, it is important to remember to record them now, as soon as we can. So carrying some sort of notebook works well for that. Later, if we want, we can transfer the write-ups into a more permanent journal or device for our own use.

A good way to record synchronicities is like this: Date; Location; Subject; Description; Conclusions. So, a hypothetical account of an incident might read something like this:

(Date); Santa Rosa, CA. Wine, Keys. We were on vacation, visiting the winsome wine country of central California. Breakfast was finished, but Rae couldn't find our rental car keys. I went down to the lobby to see if she might have dropped them there.

A couple of bottles of wine were displayed on the counter. Their labels were beautiful: charming views of the countryside there. I took a closer look at one, which happened to include the word "gardens," and flashed on a scene from yesterday. We had been sitting on a bench out back by the flowers, and Rae was holding the key..., to the end of the account.

And then the conclusions: This was a fun coincidence! Our problem was solved quickly once we started focusing on the keys. This place was so beautiful and I loved having the answer happen to come through something that agreed with my impressions of it.

And then any insights: For my writing about how to love your life: go to *places* you love, even if just for a few days. Your life is made up of days after all. There's also something going on about *gardens*. They keep coming up lately in lots of stuff. I will make a note of that symbol here.

So the concluding part of a coincidence story is a listing of your reactions to it. Put down virtually anything you feel at all. Sometimes this will be an awesome moment of insight. Other times, a thought or two, or maybe a question that has arisen. Whatever you end up with, you'll now have the stories all recorded, and your reactions to them too, for later understanding and use.

Symbols/Subject

Set up another section in your notebook to keep track of symbols. As you become more aware of coincidence, you'll observe these too. Noting the subject of each event you record makes this easier: discovering the themes that are personal to you.

It is helpful to number the synchronicities in your journal. You can then add each number to a subjects' list, and easily see which are repeating. This creates a reference, invaluable to you while writing about what you feel most, for reoccurring symbols are significant to you, even if puzzling. You can work at solving the mysterious ones later on, but it's good to record them from the start.

April, Salem, OR: I was at the library working on notes for this section about inspiration. While taking a break I found a forgotten bookmark in a novel. It was an index card with notes neatly written on both sides. On one were benefits of meditation and on the other were thoughts about receiving higher guidance. Oh! I thought when I read that. I get it. I had forgotten to list meditation as a source of inspiration, though I knew it, and used it myself. Thanks for the reminder!

As the last of our intentional sources of inspiration, meditation is a whopper. It can stimulate our ideas to write with passion. It can relax our minds so that intuition can come through. It can allow us to connect with higher guidance related to our work.

By meditation, I mean any activity that puts us in a reflective state; an altered state; an in-the-zone state of being. This can be a traditional practice of sitting to meditate, but other things as well. Anything that takes us to that mental place is meditative, and can be inspirational to our writing.

Just now: I got up to get a drink of water and check my mail.

There was a note from Deidre. She sent me a link to something she had recently read. It was a little story about getting into the flow of life by doing something that opens the mind. Exactly! Our meditative mind is an awakened and receptive mind, through which we are inspired. I love this stuff!

So back to our thread. Oftentimes a repetitive activity works well with this, encouraging a contemplative mind; actions we thoroughly know or can easily do without thinking about them. Somehow the relaxed rhythm of what we're doing allows our mind to relax and reflect.

A few common meditative activities are walking, gardening, building, and cleaning. Also observing nature and daydreaming. You can probably think of many more. We can use anything we like doing that puts us into that meditative state where our mind is relaxed and thoughtful, and open for inspiration.

Anything

I started this chapter with a question: "Where do we find our stimulus and ideas to write with passion?" And an answer: "Almost anywhere. The world is a curious and inspiring place." Though we've talked about a few great sources, you're likely to have some of your own, when you're open and attentive too.

Collect everything: ideas, images, objects—whatever. Record in your journal what makes you feel. Jot down odd or curious things that intrigue or surprise you. You may not know how to use them, or if you ever will, but they will be right there in your journal if you do. So become a collector of bits and pieces of words and thoughts and dreams, and anything else that appeals.

May, Keizer, OR: Eric and I were shopping at a local landscape supply place. We were after a few big boulders for our flowerbeds, and river rock for filler. There was an impressive selection of stone in various sizes and shapes to consider.

Eric spotted something odd. At the base of a sign of visitor rules were a couple large stones that were carved in some kind of detailed design. A closer look revealed the images to be theater comedy and tragedy masks. How strange! The symbols felt so out of place in this earthy location. I made a note in a small notebook I carried to ask about their story, and to write it down too, because it felt like there may be something more.

7: WRITING ENVIRONMENT

Environment affects our writing. The surroundings in which we work can help or hinder our goal to write with passion. Luckily, we can choose many of the conditions around us. We can select the scenery, both physical and symbolic, that will work to our own advantage.

An important standard of environment is usefulness. How beneficial is it? If the majority of surrounding things help our writing, we have chosen well. A second standard is preference. Do we like where we write? If that place, in all its many facets, feels good to us, we are more likely to do well.

Maybe because these standards are obvious, we take them for granted, don't give them much notice in the work that we do. Bu they play such a part in anything creative that we really need to do so.

A couple sentences this morning in an email from Deidre expressed the basic truth of this. "I think I need to get some housework done today," she wrote. "It is chilly out, so will be a good day to be inside."

Sounds simple, right? But here's the deal. Deidre is an avid and creative gardener who loves to work outside. All day long, often, when the weather is warm. In fact, a main reason she moved to New Mexico a few years back was to enjoy the desert's climate. So when she talks about doing housework inside instead of gardening, it's because she won't feel as good outdoors as usual, and that dampens the whole thing. And that is what I'm getting at. The same thing applies to our writing.

One way to categorize our writing environment is in terms of the equipment, tools, and location that make it up. We can then consider each of these in terms of practicality and preference. We can play with these elements, combining, adjusting, or completely changing them to come up with what works best for us. Because we perceive with our senses, we'll look at that as well, to see how our favored sense ties in with these elements.

Equipment

I think of this as any furniture or storage we use with our writing. This includes office desks, chairs, and shelves. It also includes any seating and writing surfaces in public places we might choose to work. What's important is that these things are both helpful and personally likable. Where we write needs to offer each one. If either aspect is missing—in our perspective that is—it will hamper our efforts to write with zeal.

I have trouble with chairs. A way too hard chair used years ago left me overly sensitive to them. Whenever I end up writing for the day, my seating is top priority. And I don't mind looking around for the most comfy chair. This can take a little time, like at the library where softer seats are scarce, or in a café with few booths. No matter. It pays off through finding the most usable chair for me and avoiding discomfort.

So how is the equipment in your writing area? Do your desk, chair, and any cabinets work well for you? How about any shelves or bookcases you may use? Does your furniture and storage feel like a good match, or would you like something else better? If so, you can change stuff; it's all adaptable.

While working on this section about writing environment, an email came from Deidre. There was a little write-up enclosed about the history of the pencil that her husband Adam thought I might like. I sure did—what fun! Any tidbit about the background of one of my favorite writing tools is always welcome.

Deidre and Adam both knew of my affection for good pencils, and my disgust of erasers that do not work. What they didn't know was that I was getting ready to write about the importance of tools in our writing! It's a small coincidence, but pertinent, and I read over the little story again. When I did it clicked that knowing what we do NOT like helps us know what we do. I made a note to get into this later on (and yes, you will get to hear about my pencil fetish in more detail too!).

Tools

Instruments help us do things in a favored certain way—in this case to write about what we want with passion. Devices help us do that better and easier. When it comes to our writing conditions, good tools are essential. And we get to choose them.

I think of tools as any manual or electronic implement that we consistently use to write. This includes computers, software, etc., as well as notebooks, paper, cards, and the like. It also includes tiny tools like tablet styluses, pens, and paper clips. Basically, any item that helps us do our work and enjoy it more counts as a tool.

I prefer manual tools. My final drafts and edits are done by computer on Word, but everything before that by hand. And I like to do things that way. I love paper and notebooks too much—their look, their texture, their feel—to ever give them up. They are enjoyable and effective too, so work well for my writing. This spills over also into journals, both softcover and hardback, notebooks, and cards. Any paper, really, that I find pleasing and helpful.

Pencils and erasers are my other essentials; I pretty much can't write with pens. Something to do with how hard I press down makes my words look like squiggly scratching from the tips of most pens. But the soft texture of a pencil's point is a whole different thing. It suits me, resulting in handwriting that's clear and attractive—providing that I have the *right* pencil.

So here's that deal. I only use Ticonderoga brand pencils, and buy them by the dozen. I love them and they work well for me. These beauties sharpen perfectly, are smooth and sturdy, with end erasers that really work!

And that is saying a lot. Most erasures on pencils are useless and totally annoying, simply smearing marks instead of rubbing them out. So that is what I mean by tools that help us *and* make us happy. Choose yours by both criteria.

Location

A location is a selected areas or site. In our case, a particular spot; a place where we choose to write. Locations seem to be the strongest element of our writing environment. While equipment and tools help or hamper our work, a poor location can stop it flat. We need a peaceful or lively location—whatever suits us—to reach our goals.

This may be an office at home or a place on the end of the couch, a space on the deck or a spot in the local park. We may write our best in a bustling café downtown, or a laid back library instead. But whatever place beckons, we need to go there.

Once again, our two criteria of usefulness and preference are helpful. The first is mandatory because if we choose a spot where we are unable to work, nothing happens. The second is more flexible, and I think more fun. Since both are dependent on how we take in the world, we'll dip into that.

Sight Perceptors

Approximately 60% of us are thought to be visually oriented, taking in information primarily through sight. It's how we experience and understand life—preferably. That's not to say that sight perceptors pay no attention to what they hear or feel, but that they mostly live through what they see. If that sounds like you, these aspects of your environment are important to your writing.

A major visual element is an object or place's aesthetics. Is beauty important to you? If so, writing in a place with attractive artwork, décor, or views will support your work. Colors, patterns, and designs there can play a part in the appeal too.

Small objects are another way to add touches of beauty, interest, or meaning to your environment, and can even be portable too. Begin with the do-not-likes. While it isn't necessary (and probably not possible) to get rid of every single item that bugs you, aim for the biggies. Eliminate those things that affront your visual sense. Do your best to remove the offenders.

Then add some things that you like. These might be souvenirs or symbols that hold significance for you. They will be highly personal. Objects that are appealing to someone else may not be to you, so go by feel.

To honor my preferences, I have learned to add a few objects to the places I write. One spot at home has a nearby shelf. On it is a tray of vintage bookmarks, and some copies of my first book. There are also a couple decorative boxes and a few tiny journals (love those tiny books!). Some colorful flowers complete the display. While writing, I find it pleasant and stimulating to glance occasionally at my stuff.

I sometimes work at the library instead. When I do, I often take notes in an attractive journal. And when I sit down to write I make sure to find a spot in sight of some artwork, or a window's pleasant view. This helps me to write my best, and may help you too, if you're visually oriented.

Sound Perceptors

Approximately 35% of the population are auditory, taking in information primarily through sound. It's how they experience and understand their world. Like sight perceptors, they use their other senses too, but pay more attention to what they hear, by preference.

If that seems like you, consider your writing. What kind of sound is conducive to your work? Does conversation or music in the background help you communicate your ideas? If so, at what level? Do you thrive in a bustling and noisy place? If you do, this will be paramount in deciding where to work.

Or is it the opposite? Does noise make it harder for you to work at all? In that case, a quiet and peaceful setting will be essential. Determine to find that spot, that location, that is exactly what you need.

Touch Perceptors

A small percentage of us are kinetic, taking in information primarily through touch. Though the other perceptions occur, those of touch will be preferred. If that sounds like you, things you physically feel in your environment will be important.

Furniture will be of concern; are you comfy where you write? Consider your desk or table, etc., as well as your chair. And what about lighting; is it adequate for your needs? Can you see your keyboard or paper without any strain? Though this last point is important to all of us writers, if kinetic, you may notice it more. And then there are the textures you touch, fabric and clothing in particular. Are they in any way distracting to you? Aim for overall comfort wherever you work, in all of its various forms.

And isn't that what most of us want in one way or another? A place to feel our best, however we perceive? A place to feel good enough to write about what we think about, what really matters? Positive writing places can do just that. Locate yours with care. Your work will benefit from it.

8: ORIGINALITY

April, Salem, OR: It was morning and I was driving to the library. Reaching the downtown area, I glanced at a store near the Willamette River Bridge that seemed to have been there forever. "100 Years of Service!" boasted a big sign out front.

A moment later, a delivery truck turned the corner ahead of me to go onto the bridge. "100 Years of Service!" I read once again, this time on the vehicle of a different concern. The exact repetition of the phrase appearing so quickly felt significant somehow.

A century of service? These businesses have clearly been around awhile, offering their wares, and are likely to be well-known in their fields too. My thoughts naturally move to tradition and originality, and how they play out in our writing, one versus the other.

Tradition: a practice of long standing. Beliefs and ideas passed along for some time. Originality: thinking or acting for oneself; producing something new. For to write with passion we must be our true selves, that is for sure. Share our take on our topic—our personal view. When we do this our work will be uniquely original.

But what about tradition; established concepts and views? Do they play a part in our writing as well? Or is passionate writing only the result of new ideas? I know that's not right, somehow, and would welcome more insight on it all. And as usual with the Universe, my question is heard, and answered.

As I stopped at a light, a cab pulled up in the next lane—a hot pink painted taxicab marked "Yellow Cab!" This was funny, and an example of an original idea combined with a traditional term that seemed to answer my musings. But just what was that answer? I made a mental note to record these coincidences in my journal later, and to mull over their messages.

Once at the library, I started off with a pit stop to the restroom. In the stall I found a book. Okay, it was a little creepy considering the location of the forgotten book and all, but nonetheless unusual. And because of that, I *had* to take a look. When I did (yes, after sponging the cover and washing my hands thoroughly) I saw that the title's subject was intuition, one of *my* subjects. So naturally I needed to check it out, and did so right away.

Later I found a comfy chair and fanned through the book. Author Gerd Gigerenzer's *Gut Feelings: The Intelligence of the Unconscious* looked interesting. I randomly opened the book to a section and read a few paragraphs about brand name recognition. As I did, something clicked and I intuitively understood the message of those current coincidences.

Originality in our work: we produce something unique to ourselves when we write with passion. We write about what we care about deeply. We write without copying or deriving our ideas from the personal viewpoint of others. Our words and message come alive for our readers because they are precisely our own. In short, personality equals passion.

But we all share basic concepts with a few other people anyway, so our originality is likely in the details—our particular, personal take on commonly agreed upon things. And here is where tradition supports our ideas, and helps us write with passion.

Take my first book on coincidence. Its title, *The Secret Language of Synchronicity*, is probably understandable or not understandable to an equal number of people. But its sub-title, *Deciphering the Words & Wisdom of Meaningful Coincidence*, makes it clear. Though the word "synchronicity" is a term that has become more commonly know in recent years, the word "coincidence" has been around forever, and is understood by most.

The same interplay between established and new ideas exists in the basic structure of the book. My overall definition of synchronicity is traditional, but my understanding of how it works is not. Personal experiences and study led to the discovery that different personalities experience different styles of coincidence. And this is the theme of the book.

Sub-topics throughout the book follow this pattern as well: new concepts developed from common notions. Original ideas evolved from traditional thoughts. And this is how it works. When we write with passion, our work will be centered on our unique beliefs. But will probably include some popular views. These traditional ideas will help our readers to intuit the wisdom of our original truth.

9: WRITING THEMES

Passionate writing is always possible and most probable too, once we know the prerequisites: what choices to make ahead of time before we begin. Once these are in place we're on our way to writing as we wish, with heartfelt words of meaning and power.

Choosing the main theme of our project is important as a first step. We need to clarify the idea that will run through our book. This will serve as the central subject of our non-fiction, or the plot line of our fiction, around which the topics of our chapters, or incidents of our characters revolve.

The best theme for our work is something we really care about. Something that evokes our deepest feelings. When we allow ourselves to shape our work around a strong interest or deep conviction, our passion comes right through. And is obvious to our readers.

But all this baring of the soul, even regarding seemingly non-personal subjects, involves disclosure of us as the author. For only when we write about what really matters deep inside, and how that *feels* to us, will our message and language be truly enlivened. And this can be downright scary.

January, Salem, OR: I had chosen my theme for this book, or rather it had chosen me. The message was insisting on being heard. It felt exciting and wiser than me, like being part of something far bigger than my everyday self. But the concept was unusual, going beyond the idea of intuitive guidance in writing to that of coincidental. And that made me nervous. How much was I willing to stand out from the crowd? Still, I really cared about sharing these discoveries. A group of incidents that happened to involve a free-flying symbol reassured me once more, to take the risk. It went like this:

I was taking a reading break after beginning this section. Umberto Eco, author of *Confessions of a Young Novelist*, commented within the first few pages of his title that an author's published book is sent out into the world like a message in a bottle. I stopped after reading that, the phrase seeming to stand out from the surrounding words. But why? Message in a bottle? I repeated the words a few times, trying to get a sense of any personal connotations, but didn't really get anywhere.

A bit later while reading an article online, the work "balloon" popped out at me along with an "Aha!" moment. That was it—balloons! For me writing books was almost like sending a balloon with a note attached up into the sky, to be seen by those who happen to look up, and to go wherever the wind blows. And that launching entails the concepts of courage and risk.

The coincidence of coming across another author's personal symbol had triggered an intuition about my own, when I happened upon the word "balloon," with insights about the nature of sending our deepest feelings and thoughts out there, to land wherever, and be read by whomever.

Furthermore, it seemed the existence of this association of mine was not new, but had been around awhile. I just did not recognize it yet, consciously anyway. I looked back a few months and found this in my journal:

August, Salem, OR: There was a hot air balloon floating over our house this morning. Its colors were so brilliant against the blue sky. We sometimes see them in the cool, early hours, but they aren't too common here. It is always a surprise to spot one, and a delight to watch it drift along. They remind me of something else...

Then a day later Deidre wrote that she and Adam had just visited a balloon museum. This grabbed my attention. The fact that there was such a museum near her home isn't surprising, as she lives near Albuquerque, New Mexico, site of a mammoth, extremely popular balloon festival. But it was peculiar that she was writing about it then, right after my own sighting.

I shared this with her and she responded that it got even stranger. "I just met our new neighbors," she said, "and they told me—get this—they moved here because they are hot air balloonists." Uncanny.

So what would you like your book or story to be about? What knowing do you hold down deep that it's time to share? What idea or interest do you love so much that you'd happily talk about it with others for as long as they'd listen? There is your theme.

Oftentimes our strongest passions start early. If you are stymied, you can begin the important process of choosing your theme by thinking back through the years. What things did you love to do or daydream about when you were young? Simply asking yourself the question and focusing on that will trigger answering signs.

In my own case, I started writing at eight or nine, with a couple poems about two things I love: horses and candy. Hey, what can I say? I was a kid! And I still remember those intense rhymes to this day. Yes, they were pretty bad, but the passion behind them still comes through. Then, around the same age, I discovered the metaphysics section at the library, and something I loved even more.

If you have some ideas and are considering several possible themes, you can receive guidance on that. The process is the same: first think about or research these possible topics, then focus on your question. You might ask, what is most important for me to write about now? Or, which of these themes will I enjoy writing about the most? Or simply, what should my book's theme be? Use whatever phrasing sounds best to you, mentally or aloud.

You can also receive reassurance regarding ideas you love, but are concerned to write about for one reason or another. The Universe will confirm if it's currently right for you. The following cluster of coincidences brought home for me, repeatedly, the theme most important for me to write about, and live by as well: this book's theme.

January, Salem, OR: I was starting to want to write a second book about meaningful coincidence, this one, though, about writing passionately by following intuitions and signs. I had started making some notes, but was having those same butterflies as before.

I took a break from work and began reading a new book. Randolph J. Roger's *The Key to Life: A Metaphysical Investigation* was a personal account of the author's experiences with synchronicity and past lives. It was a fascinating story, and Roger's use of the key symbol in his title and his ideas reminded me of some very different personal discoveries about unlocking synchronicity's secrets that I had made. As I read, the sight of the word felt significant somehow. I jotted down "key" and underlined it.

Over the next few days the same word and even its image kept popping up in other books I was reading. Of course, "key" is a pretty common word, but the number of times it appeared felt significant. I began playing with the term's different meanings and connotations while remaining alert for what might happen next. There was a feeling of something of importance going on.

My thoughts ran like this. Keys, first of all, are physical devices which lock and unlock, and so provide control through ownership or release. Just as often, they signify the means to something, as the access to an experience or a state. On another level keys are answers, such as logical or practical solutions. Key points provide essential facts in their role to explain.

The variations of what keys can unlock, open, or answer are unlimited. For instance, a key as a pathway to joy or success, or a guide to needed information. Or as a cipher for unlocking things hidden, as in mysterious codes. In this case, the key is what's needed to click open the door to secret knowledge or words.

A bit later my thoughts were still running over these associations as I prepared to go for a walk. I zipped up my jacket and reached in the pocket, where I came across—a key. Okay, no big deal—but the timing was odd. This particular key had been lost for many months. But it turned up right then, as if to say, hey—pay attention! Here is the key! I was delighted by the coincidence, and looked forward to what might be next.

I didn't have long to wait. Remembering a book at the library in which the key symbol played an essential role, I decided to do some sleuthing. In *The Essential Lenormand: Your Guide to Precise & Practical Fortunetelling*, author Rana George taught a divination system for prediction and insight. I located the book, pulled up a chair, and dug in, discovering that it used a card deck illustrated with simple objects, including the key. The book explored divinatory layouts as well as meanings of individual cards. I zeroed in on the key section.

George's discussion of key symbolism included some familiar associations, as well as others unique to the Lenormand. Some meanings were precisely pertinent to the focus of my work. I still didn't understand the message of the key synchronicities for me, but felt that I soon would. Things were lining up too well.

Further on in the book I came across something that jumped right out. It was a drawing of a large key with this written on it: "Flow is the Key." Immediately I got goose-bumps, recognizing the personal message of these words. Though the author was using them in a certain way unique to her subject, they said something different to me, as reassurance about the rightness of this book's theme.

But what was that message? As I studied the drawing and its curious words it suddenly clicked. *Flow* is the *Key* to synchronicity. When we intuitively follow what feels best to do we flow. And the Universe responds through coincidental help. And that pertains to our writing as well. When we choose to write about what we really care about, we are supported every step of the way, and passionate books are the result.

It was early morning, a few days after these key incidents. A new neighbor had moved in next door. She appeared at our door, visibly shaken, dressed in nightgown and robe. "I've locked myself out of the house," she exclaimed, "and this new key doesn't work!"

Eric went over for a look and got the door opened. Later he took a bike ride while I was in town. Then, back home he found that he had taken along the wrong key and was locked out!

Meanwhile, at the library, I was busy searching for something on the history of the same objects. I thoroughly checked the shelves, but the book I was after was missing. A woman nearby asked about it.

I told her, and she broke into a grin. "That's funny," she said, "because my husband and I *collect* old keys. We pull them up from the shallows of Lake Detroit with a metal detector. The entire town was moved, you know, when they built the dam."

No, I really didn't, so asked her when that was. "In the 1950s, but we find keys from much earlier than that. Underneath the water are parts of an old 1800s railroad line, and the original town of Detroit." Fascinating.

So the message was still repeating through the appearance of the keys, to make sure I got it. *Flow* is the *key*. Lost keys, found keys, real and symbolic, old keys and new. It felt like a lesson I was meant to remember. And I did. The string of coincidences caught my attention so much that I have started a collection of old keys myself, as fun reminders!

It is useful to write out the theme for your book in a sentence or two. What is this important thing you really want to share? Go ahead and write it down, that central thread. Just doing that in itself will be helpful.

I like to write my theme on the first page of a notebook. Seeing it often while I work reminds me of its role, and ensures that I choose topics to include that play a part in its message. Writing down your theme will do the same, whether on paper or the computer, and start you on your path to your goal of passionate writing.

Titles

Choosing titles for your books is an important part of your writing. Titles tell what your books are about. With a great title, readers who like your kind of story will be drawn to it. And that's what we want: readers who will enjoy our stories when they buy and read our books. But what makes a great title, anyway?

I think of a title as a concise summary of a book's main theme. Oftentimes a sub-title is added to clarify an attention-getting short title. Between the two, readers should get a clear idea of what the book is about. Sometimes a title tells about the main theme with words that portray its overall mood, or location, or characters, instead of its action or subject; whatever element the author feels is strongest in the book, and wants to stress.

Every key word in our title needs to be essential. We want their meaning to be instantly clear. A few words might be all that's needed, or a much longer string. We've all come across books with titles that were so enticing that we had to take a closer look. And the opposite too, titles that were boring or dull. So adding color as well as clarity is good. Overall we want the feel of our title to match that of our book, as well as be enticing and clear.

The sound of a title affects its value as well. Smoothness and rhythm will go a long way. Listening to the sound of our selections will help us choose the best one. It's really just a matter of reading your possible titles to see if they flow, and have the feel you want to convey.

When I was creating this book's title, I knew its basic words of "writing" and "coincidence," which comprised my theme. At first I tried "Book Writing by Coincidence," but it didn't have the punch of the shorter phrase, "Writing—by Coincidence."

And then there's the dash in the title. That idea came to me after I had the initial three words, and it worked really well, because what makes this book different from others is that second part about coincidence. So putting in the pause through the dash goes along with how we might think when reading the title. It's a book on writing, but more: writing that's helped by coincidence.

The subtitle was trickier. I knew I needed it to add to the first three words about the goal to write with passion. And I wanted the words "signs" and "synchronicity" in it too. Also, since "flow" is an important part of the theme, I hoped to include that word too. Initially the subtitle began with "following," which I later changed to "flowing," and then the whole thing came together well.

Your title should be as unique as the book it describes. Let your inner voice help you choose its words. And be open for tips from the big U that may apply. Doing this will lead you to the best title for you work that summarizes how you feel.

10: EXCITEMENT

March, Salem, OR: It was early morning and I was pretty excited. The day was the start of a sale on my first book, *The Secret Language of Synchronicity*. I really didn't know what to expect, having not run one of these count-down deals through Amazon before. But I was hopeful for what its results might be.

A promo can increase an author's visibility online, along with accompanying sales: more people reading their ideas and work. What felt best, to me anyway, was the chance to connect, to talk, and share my passions with others. And that was what I was hoping for there, to be able to do more of that, thanks to the deal.

So I turned on the computer to look at my stats, and was happy to find extra sales, then checked back often while puttering around, getting ready for my day. And during this the thought kept popping up that excitement, like I was feeling then, was an essential part of being able to write with passion and enjoy it.

About this time I received something in the mail from a friend. It was a St. Patrick's Day card in a charming design. The shamrocks on the front reminded me right off of my book I was just promoting, with its four-leaf clover on the cover. The verse mentioned sweet moments and simply joys, and sent wishes for fun, reflecting the feeling of the current day.

Excitement. Things that thrill us and stir up our emotions. Ideas, values, stories, whatever, that offer powerful pleasure and joy. Themes or plots that inflame and delight us. Yes, we can write passionately about what invokes positive feelings, or the opposite, negative ones. But my experience and the thrust of this book are on the former.

So sharing what excites us, what awakens our deep emotions, is key to writing that will touch our readers. It is the most important thing, I think, for us to do. But being an author, and our work itself, offer other excitement options too, that will keep our writing stimulating and personally true.

One of the most exciting things about being an author is having the freedom to write about what we care about. As long as our themes are not injurious to others, the fields are wide open. It is thrilling to be able to focus our writing on the interests and ideas that enliven us and make us who we are.

It is also exciting to bring pleasure to our readers, while doing what we enjoy. Our heartfelt words can entertain, teach, or even serve as stepping-stones on someone's personal path. We never know which of our insights may guide another to exactly what they need to see at a particular moment.

As I was working on this section, a friend who buys and resells stereo equipment as a hobby stopped by. He was thrilled by a recent transaction, and that he now could "make space" for other finds. The whole process was exciting to him, from discovering a quality piece, to researching its value, to selling it to an appreciative customer. And naturally he wanted to do more. And he could. Making physical space for doing what he loved provided him with the mental clearance he needed to go ahead.

And this works the same with our writing. We need physical space of some kind that is conducive to our work, and we need the mental space as well: an empty place free of distracting thoughts where we allow ourselves to focus on what is exciting, and share it through our words.

The financial part of writing with passion is exciting too. Once we learn to follow the flow of intuitions and signs, our writing really comes alive. We write about what matters most to us, and our feelings come through, resulting in emotional experiences for readers. Now we have the opportunity to earn our income doing what we love to do, writing with spirit.

Publishing options of today can add to our excitement, and therefore our success, in doing what we want to do. We can keep control of most aspects of the books we write, including profit margin, by going the indie route of self-publishing. Or we can choose a traditional approach instead. Whatever options concerning the business side of our writing that feel the most exciting are our best choices.

Probably the most exciting thing about writing with passion is being able to dwell in that deep feeling place. Through our work we can talk about what we care about, what we already know. But it goes beyond that. Writing with the guidance of coincidence leads to learning more about our theme, and our personal potential too. Now that's exciting!

11: WRITING TOPICS

Creating a tentative topics list works well after coming up with your title. This will be a rough idea of chapter subjects for your book. It will also serve as a flexible outline that will provide direction as you write.

"Tentative" is the keyword here because your plans are likely to change. You will spontaneously come up with new topics you want to include. Coincidences that you experience along the way will be meaningful and suggest additional subjects. The Universe will lead you to ideas that resonate deeply within and need to be part of your book.

Begin by jotting down topics you know you want to include. A notebook works well for this. After your initial session, keep adding to your list for a few days as more topics occur to you, or as more details about the ones you have already written down arise.

Meanwhile, stay alert for inner or outer signs. These intuitions and coincidences will confirm, clarify, or add to the choices you are making. Your thoughts about what is important to include will trigger answers in the form of synchronicities that are right for you, like this:

January, Salem, OR: I was at the big Goodwill store, one of my favorite places to shop, and to sometimes experience synchronicity too. You never knew what you would find in these places, and the search was always fun, and occasionally enlightening.

Their aisles of knick-knacks were color-coded. There were sections of red-, yellow-, blue-, and green-colored objects. Purple and pink had their special areas too, as did items of black or white, all organized neatly to appeal to shoppers.

On the back of a top shelf of a display of cups I spotted something different. It was a painting, clearly out of place. Someone, I thought, had probably carried it around awhile then put it back up there. I was curious, and took the picture down for a closer look.

The painting was small; an original watercolor, about 10"x12" in size. There was no artist signature or frame. The image was unusual: a golden bee and a creamy white flower, with evergreen trees in front and a snowy mountain behind. Curving across the top in script were two words, a surname and "Honey."

I was strangely drawn to the picture. Though not sure what it was all about, I was sure that I wanted it. So I bought it for some change and took it home. I was also certain that it tied in somehow with the Topics section of this book I was working on then.

The first thing that sprang to mind about the image was the setting of the scene. Mr. Bee and his flower looked a little lost out there in the wilderness. But what freedom! A forest stretched in front of them, and a mountain peak rose behind. He could gather his nectar wherever.

And then it hit me. Independence in creativity—that's what this was about. Here was a subject of utmost importance to me: the state of freedom, so necessary to be able to write with passion. Thanks to the big U and the strange little picture I happened to find, I wouldn't forget to include this topic.

Oh, yeah. I *had* to check out the background of the painting. Turned out that an apiary out near Silverton, a pretty little town near waterfalls and hills, had once sold honey. The little watercolor with the bee by Mt. Hood may have been created for its labels—artwork that ended up a treasure for me.

So, getting back to our tentative list, you will be able to add, subtract, or alter topics at any point, depending on how they feel to you. The final form of your book's content, however, will only evolve by the end of your project, for writing passionately in flow, using the skills of intellect guided by Spirit, will likely result in many ongoing changes.

February, Rickreal, OR: Three of us, my husband Eric, our friend Dan, and I were at a nearby flea market. It was held once a month, and was very popular. A mixture of antiques, hand-crafted, and just plain strange stuff drew an excited crowd. We joined the throng at the door.

Inside we split up and went our separate ways. The market consisted of three large rooms full of wares. So I made a beeline over to one edge, planning to zigzag across the whole thing.

I had only covered a few tables when something caught my attention.

It was a small lacquer box. The background finish was shiny black with an intricate painted design. Delicate peach and amber buildings were outlined in metallic gold, and sat among lacy trees. A little snow covered the ground. The architecture and setting images looked Russian to me, but I was not sure. The little box was pretty and priced fairly, so I bought it.

A few aisles later, I came upon a box of old papers, a particular fondness of mine. I pretty much am charmed by any unusual found paper. But vintage ads, cards, and such hold an extra appeal, and I buy a few pieces here and there. This time I ended up with three seemingly unrelated items: a couple late 19th century bookmarks, and a 1950s ink blotter. I looked forward to later checking out the history of my finds.

Later, I was working on this section, and got the urge to study these latest finds. There was a vague but persistent feeling of something I needed to recall. Nothing might come of it, as not every word or image we see is a sign for us. But some are, and announce themselves through subtle sensations.

I stopped what I was writing to consider the four flea market items. The little box was lovely, but brought up no feelings of anything more. One of the antique bookmarks advertised kitchen ranges and pictured a young girl in period dress. The other advertised a steam laundry, with a sailboat theme. Neither the words nor the images of either bookmark brought up anything related to this project at all. But the last piece, the 1950s calendar-blotter, did.

It was an advertising giveaway for a florist in Olympia, Washington. "Flowerplace 8, Opposite to Liberty Theatre," it explained, with "P.S. We Telegraph Flowers." There was a fresh-looking arrangement pictured with "Gay Spring Flowers Brighten Any Occasion," plus a small calendar of the month of April.

Altogether I was reminded of warmth and pleasure, and how feeling good about our subject and excited about possibilities plays a major part in writing with zeal. I made a note of these topics, excitement and possibility, to include in this book (which I did).

Once your list is done you are ready to make an outline. Each of your topics can be a chapter in itself. Or you can combine them, several subjects that go well together, into different chapters. I like to do this step by hand, as I do all preliminary writing steps, but by computer works fine too. Either way will allow you to organize your material.

Some authors outline extensively, some moderately, and some not at all. I have found that this loose form of a tentative list works best when writing in flow. Serving as a roadmap of your project, the outline will show your route, yet be open to vital detours and discoveries, or subject side trips that beckon to you. And that is essential.

Sometimes while working on your outline (or any other part of your book) a confusing coincidence will occur. I think of these puzzles as mystery messages. Because of their timing and feeling, you will recognize them as related to your writing somehow; you just won't know how. Be sure to record them anyway; in time you probably will.

February, Applegate, OR: I was in the middle of writing this section when my friend Amy was in a car accident. No one was hurt, but both cars were damaged. She emailed me and said, "A few days after the accident I was worried that the witness to the accident would be hard to contact. Her cell phone was an eastern area code.

"I decided to clean out a magazine rack which was really stuffed and had several Jacksonville newspapers in it that I didn't think I had read. So I opened up the first one to see, and on the page it opened to was the witness's name in bold. Turns out that she and her husband had recently opened a shop in town, and also lived next door to one of the vineyards on my road."

What a helpful coincidence! Amy needed that info, and she needed it soon. Feeling the urge—right then for some reason—to weed out an overstuffed magazine rack paid off. There was the important name and address in a paper, printed in bold lettering to boot.

And was there a message in the story for me too? Amy knows

that coincidence is my subject, so there is always that. And she sometimes tells me her incidents. But the timing of this event suggested a link with my current writing too, so I added "unlimited connections" to my Topics list.

This theme of limitlessness, this time between people, was repeated the next day through Deidre, my friend. She told of an uncannily arranged connection between her daughter and her son, who live hundreds of miles apart. She wrote:

"Sara and Sean are in Cozumel for a week of scuba diving. Jack is playing a cruise ship gig, and will be, coincidentally, in Cozumel tomorrow. So he'll get to see Sara. Small world indeed. Jack hasn't done a cruise ship gig in years, but he's playing with a bunch of people he's played with over the years."

The topics of your list will be the contents of your outline. You can write each topic down on a separate index card. Below each one, list any subtopics, and leave some extra space for details and new ideas that may come up while you are writing.

The last step of your outline is to put the topics into the order you want them to appear in your book. Having all their cards displayed in front of you makes this easier. What topics need to be covered first before others make sense? What subject (or scene) feels most important to begin your book? And what topics, subtopics, or details from different cards would work really well together, now that you consider it?

Go ahead and play with this. Move your cards around or cut them up and recombine them if you want. Let your intuition guide you to new connections between your topics or ideas. Jot things down on your cards if inclined. Keep your focus on coming up with an order that will flow for reading, and for writing. After awhile, when nothing else seems to come, copy down your outline in as much detail as feels right to do.

You now have a structure in place for your book. Its outline is flexible, as new ideas are likely to come through your thoughts and ideas. If you remain open and alert, changes may be suggested through coincidental messages too. But most importantly, you now have a map in place to guide you toward your goals.

12: FOUND OBJECTS

Found Objects. Curiosities we come across by coincidence. Paper pieces that we light upon by chance. Items that we discover, of value or not, that hold meaning for us. Messages conveyed through strange or forgotten things are some of the most fun synchronicities we'll have. Because like the old adage goes, you never know what you'll find.

I personally have received guidance through objects as diverse as a playing card, an antique letter, and an old dollar bill. Forgotten bookmarks of all sorts and sizes are big with me. But then I'm a paper person and a vintage buff besides, and the Universe does aim to please.

Found object synchronicities that help us write can be weird and wonderful. Some coincidental gems that brighten our path are like sparkly stones. I think of these beauties as wave-tossed bits on a beach that beckon and shine. Sometimes they turn out to be glass polished smooth by the sea, and sometimes tumbled stones. All are worth collecting.

What sets these apart from similar signs is precisely their light. They seem to sparkle somehow, to catch our eye. Though we don't see this literally, we feel it, when we come upon them, when we experience their glow. And that's the odd thing about them. They are easy to spot—a dropped object, forgotten scrap, whatever—because of their feel. And we don't know why, what any of it means at all. But if we will flow with that feeling as best we can wherever it leads, we may find out.

March, Salem, OR: It was morning and I was browsing in a secondhand store I hadn't been to for awhile. It was something I always enjoyed (big surprise, right?) and a fun break from writing. The shop was brimming with lots of small stuff, my favorite kind of wares. It reminded me of the Found Objects section of the book I was working on.

In a storage bin of small journals and assorted bound paper, I found a tiny hardback book. *Climbing Roses* was all that was stamped in gold on the dark green cover. For some reason the sight of this little book sent chills down my spine. I wonder what's up with that, I thought to myself.

I looked inside the book. Most pages featured a color photo of a type of climbing rose, its characteristics, and a description of the flower. I read one and was immediately drawn in to that place. The author's words carried his feelings for his subject so well, in witty and affectionate prose. They made the roses seem so—well, real. The write-ups were so charming in just a paragraph or two that it made me want to plant some roses!

And that was odd, because I really don't like roses all that much in comparison to other flowers. Their scent is divine and their blossoms bountiful. But I like the foliage and thorn-free stems of other plants better. Even so, the little book stood out for some reason or another, and I knew better than to argue with that. I paid for it pronto and took it home.

A few days later, a book I once read sprang to mind, and I looked it up again. It wonderful title is: *In Search of Lost Roses: through ghost towns, graveyards, wildernesses, backyards—an intrepid gardener joins the quest for the great old roses of the past*, and its author is Thomas Christopher.

The book tells the fascinating story of a worldwide rescue of old roses that nearly disappeared in the 1800s, with the raising of hybrid tea roses. I was drawn to the unusual treasure hunt tale the first time I read it, and seemed to be again. Something to do, it seemed, with the new little book on roses.

When I picked up *In Search of Old Roses*, I noticed a new book out by Elizabeth Gilbert, entitled *Big Magic: Creative Living Beyond Fear*. It sounded interesting, so I opened the book to take a look. When I did I was so surprised. In a section entitled "The Scavenger Hunt," the author tells a personal story about a passionate interest, botanical history, writing, and coincidence!

Oh, I saw then that this wasn't about those authors at all. My trail of connections had been meant for this book, arranged to show how found objects can be sensational signs for our writing, as well as an example of how that works.

Where then do we find these objects that are meant as signs for us? Pretty much anywhere that we hang out. Places we enjoy spending time are most likely. When we focus on writing about what we care about, the Universe may help through the symbolism of objects. It's always to our advantage to watch for these fun forms of coincidence.

13: WRITING SCHEDULES

How often and when should we write? And do we need a schedule? These are important questions about the writing we want to do. And like all aspects of it, there is no one-size-fits-all. Our approach will be based on ourselves and the process itself.

What works well is a tentative plan, like we create for the outline of our book. A timetable that will give us a place to start. Once into our project, we can tweak or adjust it, depending on how it feels. The main thing is to set up something we can play with.

Begin by choosing a certain time of the day to write. Consider: are you a morning, an afternoon, or a night person? When are you at your best? When do you have some free time to write, or at least some potential free time to possibly do so? Go by your intuition here in setting up your plan. Remember, it's changeable.

How often do you want to write? Every day or a few times a week? Or does once or twice a month sound better? There are no best answers here, so go by what seems right, and add frequency to your tentative schedule.

How exclusively do you like to work? With one task or with several? Which way of working is most natural for you? Single- or multi-tasking is another aspect of your tentative schedule to think about. Just making these personal choices will help you get underway with your writing.

After writing the last sentence, I took a break to check my email. There was a message from my friend Deidre. She told me about a book I might like that centered on a historical key. Deidre knows my fascination with keys, and the coincidences I've had involving them. So letting me know about the book wasn't surprising.

What was though was the timing, right at the point I'd been thinking about how synchronicities interact with our writing schedule. It seemed I'd been reminded once again of my earlier insight, that flow is the key: the key to experiencing coincidental help with every aspect of our work, including its timetable.

So once our schedule is in place, we have a working plan. We've chosen when and how often to write. From here on it's a matter of being alert for messages about our decision. There may be suggestions to help us improve our schedule, making it more beneficial for us. There may be ideas about its ease or its use. Or there may be coincidences that lead us to aspects we haven't yet considered—like breaks.

While writing this last sentence, I had an urge to look at some old (are you ready for this?) matchbooks. Let me back up a bit. A week or so earlier I was looking around a ritzy resale shop. It was a fun place to browse, with free coffee and cookies to boot, and the profits went to a couple good charities. Their merchandise was pretty high-end and spendy though. Even so, I occasionally found some odd and appealing item priced below their normal classy stuff.

Anyway, in an out-of-the-way spot I came upon an older book with "Matchbook Cover Album" on the front. Curious, I had to take a look. When I did I found page after page full of vintage matchbook covers from the 1950s and on. They were colorful and clever with wonderfully detailed graphics and ads. Some were funny, and all were fun; so fun that I bought them all.

So back to our story. I took out a small stack of covers that were not yet mounted in the book. Looking through them, I locked onto one that really stood out. "Owl Club," it advertised. "Café, Cocktails, Casino. Battle Mountain, Nevada." Then on the other side a silver nightscape glowed against midnight blue with the words, "Open all night."

This immediately brought to mind the owls among us who write. Those who don't mind the dark like Mr. Owl. Was this their perfect schedule then, working straight through the night? I didn't think so. The "all night" part of the boast bothered me. No matter when we write, each of us need breaks in our work to rest and relax. The key was determining what kind.

We can approach this the same way as our schedule; make a plan and see how it goes, then be open for anything that has to do with our breaks. Here are some personal differences that may affect what kind break will work best for you.

How often: If we prefer working for blocks of time, we'll likely not take many breaks. Finishing a certain part of our writing will probably work better. But if we like to multi-task on several things together, frequent breaks will do the trick. These periods of not working will provide just what we need.

I'm a multi-tasker. Though I've often wondered if being left-handed with right-brain tendencies has anything to do with it, the bottom line is it works. For me, that is. As long as I work in short springs between several things at the same time I'm happy. And things get done. But plodding along on something for a big block of time is blah and boring, and usually unfinished as well.

Just a few minutes ago: Eric came in from outside and asked if I'd like to go for a walk. "Sure," I said, and we headed out. It was a clear and bright day, and spring was in the air. Though our nights were still chilly, people were cleaning up flowerbeds and putting in new plants. It was inspiring. "Should we start in on that new bed out front?" I suggested.

"No, I don't want to right now. Whatever you want to do though is great. I need to finish the banisters on the deck before starting another project." Voila! My hardworking single-tasking husband had just voiced the alternate approach—coincidentally. One thing at a time until done, with few distracting breaks, was his method.

When: The time of our breaks depends on their frequency. If we single-task and write by sections, we probably won't be comfortable taking too many breaks until we finish a particular part. If we multi-task, we are likely to go more by our attention span. When I write, a feeling of discontent comes up when I need to take a break and do something different. Even if it's just for a minute or two, a short break from writing restores my focus.

What kind: The type of our breaks will depend on our current needs. Is a short diversion from writing all we're after? Then a brief break doing anything different should work. Like dishes or petting the cat—whatever. Or do we need a stretch to really relax and renew? Then a longer restful break is due. Follow your energy on this. Ideal types of breaks will come to mind when you mentally or physically need them.

The little stack of old matchbook covers was still sitting on a nearby table. I picked it up and thumbed through it again. This time one with cute little drawings of buses and people called out.

"Comfort ride," it boasted. "The best way to the finest through service to all 48 states!" And there we had it. Take care of our needs and reach our goals wherever they may lead—in the smoothest way possible.

14: WRITING SPEED

How fast should we write with spirit? As fast or as slow as it goes. For each of us, writing speed will depend upon differences of our natures and our lives. There is a pace to discover that is perfect to work in flow with passion. We need to find that personal pace.

Before we can even begin to work, we need the strength to do so; the vitality to be able to think and feel. We must have the energy available upfront to write about deep concerns, or nothing will happen at all. A quick little coincidence this morning reminded me of this truth.

I was in the kitchen doing dishes. Suddenly the water pressure dropped way down, with just a trickle coming through. I turned off the faucet. A few minutes went by, during which I retried the tap a couple of times. All at once the water surged back out. Eric came in from outside where he had been talking with a neighbor. He said that a water line had broken and just now was repaired, restoring the water's full force. What an apt reminder to keep our own force flowing, for writing and well-being.

Our own rhythm—the personal pace in which we think, speak, and act—is the first big factor that affects our writing speed.

This is our optimum rate of being. When we try to push beyond the natural range that is right for us, it simply doesn't work. This doesn't mean that we should never stretch ourselves beyond our comfort levels, including that of our writing. Just to do so gently at our normal pace. Eric shed light on this when he happened to make a comment about something totally different.

I was thinking about this topic of writing speed when my husband came into the room. He walked over to me, and then glanced down at some dumbbells in his hands. "These new weights I got are just not working," he said.

"What's the matter with them?"

"They're just too heavy. I wanted to increase the weights I'm lifting, but went too far. I need to do it in smaller increments." Ah, I think, just like writing. We need to stretch gradually, but within our range, or the whole thing will not work. Reach—but gently—at our own personal pace.

Another factor that may affect the speed we write is our working environment. Though we've explored the details of the places where we write, it's worth mentioning here that lack of an optimum spot to work can slow us down, or even halt our writing altogether. But that's something we can remedy fairly easily.

And then there's our life itself. What is currently going on with other people and events that can affect our writing? Because any other part of our life may help or hinder our work. Thankfully, when we learn to write in flow, being guided by coincidence, these factors will be more than compensated for by the Universe. We will be in the best place to write, at the ideal pace, aided by the big U.

Our deep writing is a joint venture between our intuitive self and Spirit. When we're in the zone and feel it, our work will flow. We'll write at a speed just right, focusing on intent and watching for clues. But we can't hurry it. There will be inner and outer signs to consider, and adjustments to make, when we write with passion.

15: SECRETS

Secrets. We all have them. Things that are private, thoughts that we hide, feelings we conceal. Parts of ourselves that we choose to keep that way, to ourselves. And yet to write with passion, to enliven our words and thoughts on the page, we need to share our secrets.

If readers are to feel the spirit of our ideas, we must write from where it resides: from our place of secrets. We must look for our secrets and bravely offer them up in our books. But where exactly is that place?

March, Lincoln City, OR: Eric and I were at the beach, browsing in a gallery. There was a good assortment of art in the front rooms of the shop. A back room held the work of students, plus sale items. I began thumbing through a bin holding prints of original paintings, when a picture grabbed my attention.

It was a simple scene, a secluded pool edged by grass and big stones. Thick foliage hid the pool, and a few trees outlined it, their reflections rich and dark. Colors and the air itself looked soft, surrounding water clear and deep.

I flipped the picture over and found the scene's title, "Secret Pond." This immediately brought up associations with the subject of this book. Writing with passion, I thought, is like diving deep into our own waters, bringing up treasures to share. We offer what's heartfelt, meaningful to us, from that secret place. This insight felt so right that I went ahead and bought the picture as a pleasant reminder.

Interestingly, my intuition was soon clarified. Details were added to complete the idea. It seemed that another sign was needed to make sure I understood the whole message for me. It was the next day, and I was moseying around the library, enjoying the crafts section, when I came upon a forgotten bookmark in a title on collage. I pulled the paper from the book to look at what was there, and took a second look. What?

I was flat out flabbergasted, and couldn't believe what I read. What someone, a stranger, chose to disclose. What intimate secret someone chose to tell about them self, and leave within a book—by accident? I thought so, probably, but then why did they even write down what they did in the first place? Must have had some reason or another.

Then, moving beyond these thoughts, there was a click of understanding. Oh, secrets, disclosure and passionate writing. The things with deep meaning we share in our books are the subjects we write about. But not *everything* else that's personal. We share the deep feelings about the themes of our writing, but not our entire lives! We all know that.

So what it gets down to then, is writing what we feel; reaching out with our words to tell what is within. Telling those secrets about our chosen theme through personal and passionate words. For our secrets do hold power, and those that are meant to be told will insist upon it.

16: FIRST DRAFTS

Here you are, ready to begin writing about something you feel deeply, a book or story that you're inspired to share. Seems kind of daunting, doesn't it? With so many options, deciding where to start can be confusing. Even with an outline in place, it's just so, well, wide open!

When should you start, and where? And how do you watch for guidance plus keep things moving along? Like each step of this process, there are no set rules, but ways that work very well. Before exploring these, let's consider final drafts a minute.

What is a first draft anyway? From my way of thinking, first drafts are our first written words; the initial works that come to mind as we start our story. And as such they are important as well as crucial, for first drafts serve not only to express our deep feelings, but to capture them too, providing something to work with later.

But first drafts are much more than this. They are the start of our creative writing journey. A trip that may take us to places unknown. And that journey, when guided by coincidence, will help us write and share with passion. Even so, taking the first step of that way we long to go can be stressful and downright scary. Creating involves letting go of our fears and bushwhacking a trail of our own. And that always holds risk and requires courage.

June, Keizer, OR: I had taken the day off from work, at this point of writing about risk and courage. Deidre emailed me a confirming little story. She explained, "I took Natalie to our favorite pub today. She'd never been there, and is not a beer drinker. I introduced her to oatmeal stout and now have a beer convert!"

Reading this, I immediately remembered my friend once quietly telling someone who was making a face while looking at a new dish to be brave and taste it before scowling. Exactly. We've got to take that first step, and take a chance, to get where we want to go.

Metaphors can be helpful to our process. Collage is a visual metaphor for our writing that is helpful to me. Sometimes I find it easier to stay on track and in flow by comparing the two. Doing that, I find that both arts involve collecting, affixing, and arranging to create a pleasing form.

Collecting in collage is the gathering of images. In writing it is ideas that we save. While collage uses objects in its art form, we use words. Our collecting is made up of thoughts, feelings, insights, observations, and anything else we note before writing.

Affixing in collage is gluing down elements, and in writing it's putting down words, which will evolve over time into our first draft. We really can't make mistakes at this step; everything written has worth, even parts that don't seem to work at all. We can always change these later, and sometimes, better yet, they lead to insights.

Three days ago: I wanted to talk about collage in this section on first drafts, since its metaphor is helpful to me. But I wasn't sure how to do it. So I picked up some books to research, always fun to do, and took a lot of notes. Then I wrote a few pages on the art. But the whole bit was off; I could feel it. And I didn't know how to fix it. And nothing was moving along. So I erased the entire thing and went on with my topic—kind of. By the end of the day it was clear that I'd gone too far. Here's what happened.

I came across an interesting library book. (I know, I know, something new—but wait.) The author, an artist, had written about another art form as a metaphor to his own. Written an *entire* book. It made a fascinating theme, that the author was passionate about, for an entire book's length of pages.

With that fact in front of me, I right away knew the trouble with my own little section; too much detail veering away from my theme. Collage had been written up playing the star instead of a supporting role. And that's certainly not what I had in mind when I started! So the message that came through was clear. By all means tell about the actors, but remember who is running the show, by chance.

Metaphors: use them or not as you like. If a visual image for writing in flow or for writing steps is helpful, give them a whirl. Or try some based on sound if you prefer. My stream metaphor for flow, and collage metaphor for writing, have helped keep the big pictures in mind. Some might do the same thing for you. Play around with if you feel inclined.

Now, getting back to our process. Our first step is always to stay attuned. Sometimes this is always a cinch; other times not so much. But *writing* in flow means *being* in flow, so that is where we start. I have a private phrase that helps with this. It's helpful to repeat it to myself now and then throughout the day, as a reminder of my part of the bargain. Sometimes, though, I do forget.

Two days ago: Deidre emailed me and mentioned how well her meditation practice was going. She explained that she was experimenting with a koan, or personally meaningful phrase. Check.

Then the question again is how do we know it's the right time to begin our book? We don't really. At least we don't in some this-is-absolutely-the-correct-answer kind of way. Like with all the earlier steps of our writing process, we go by feel.

Are you inspired by your topic, and excited to get going, even if nervous about it too? Do you have some kind of outline or tentative plan in place? If so, chances are the time is right for you now.

Where should you start? Wherever seems most fun! You can write your book in any order whatever. The important thing is to follow your energy on this. Begin your writing session for the day at the place you most want to be in your story. Begin where you are most anxious to share what you feel.

Why do this? Because it works well as a way to ease into flow, a way that is simple and pleasant besides. A way to the path of the work where you want to go. And to the first steps of your first draft that will ultimately get you there.

For fiction, you might choose to start at the beginning of the story or at a certain chapter instead. Or maybe at a particular incident or description. There might be a conversation half-written in your mind that you're anxious to get down instead. Wherever is most appealing is where you should start.

For non-fiction, you might start at the beginning too, or any other place. Particular chapters or sub-topics may pull you in. Or even a sub-sub-topic (if there is such a term) like I am writing now. It doesn't matter where you start, as long as you do every time.

By "every time," I mean each time you write, whether that's

multiple times a day, a week, or whatever. Though it might be confusing to change topics every few minutes, if that's the length of your sprints between breaks, even that is doable. And a few times a day, no problem at all. Alternately, if starting a certain section and staying with it until it is done feels best, do that.

Take breaks during your writing as needed. Use varying activities or environments during them to maintain interest in your work. Often just a short spell doing, seeing, or hearing something different than your writing is all that's needed to allow you to return to work refreshed and eager to go.

Longer breaks are important too, so take them when you want to, when they're the only thing you know you want to do. Take a day, a week, or whatever to get away in some manner to rest and renew. This should help you get back in sync to where you want to be: writing your first draft.

How should you write these first words, this first vision of your story? The same way you naturally thing and speak. With this simple guideline your personal voice will come through. And that's what you want, to tell your take about what matters to you most, to write with meaning and zeal. And talking to your readers on paper like you speak will do that.

What about editing; should you revise as you go, or wait until you're done? Should you correct and alter what you have written all along the way? It seems to work best when writing in flow to edit as little as possible, to keep your story moving the very best you can. There will be ample time to smooth and simplify your thoughts later on.

Affecting that though is your comfort level; how good these words must be for you to work and write in peace. There is no point in trying to push on if what you've just written feels wrong. So experiment with the process by writing and rereading and a little revising too, while aiming to let your true self come through.

As a final point, it is helpful for us to remember that our goal to stay in sync while writing is really no different than doing so with other writing steps. It can take a little more juggling though. We need to focus on writing our first draft while also staying alert for inner and outer signs, and then to follow those promptings when they occur.

This can feel annoying (hey, I'm busy here…) if we're impatient, but nonetheless should be done. After all, isn't that what this is all about? And usually leads to—I promise—much better things. Things that will help us find our voice, and write deeply what we feel. So, as you start your first draft, be prepared for some juggling, which I'm sure you'll be better at than me!

Yesterday, Salem, OR: I visited my mom to see how she was doing, and to sit and talk awhile. We did that, and then I saw one of those coloring books for adults lying around. I asked her about it, and she was a little confused, but knew that it had been a gift. I found the accompanying box of pencils and set us up. Then we enjoyed ourselves, coloring together for awhile.

Here's the point. This lady had been an artist in younger years. She painted gorgeous flowers and quilted intricate covers for family and friends. Her entire apartment where she lived now was decorated with her colorful artwork. But she couldn't do it anymore. Her manual dexterity was gone and it was just too hard.

Yet she was still an artist—inside anyway—with her passion for portraying beautiful flowers. So as we randomly colored away on our picture of abstract blossoms, she said we should have picked a color scheme, and had me fill in the white spots she couldn't help leaving behind. And yes, if you're wondering, she really enjoyed dipping into this bit of art again!

Then a while later, when I got back to writing this section, the whole incident kept coming to mind, butting into the flow of my thoughts, and kept on until I thought, okay, and stopped, and went and did some other things while thinking about the coloring. And then the simple insight came that if we will just put down some words, and work on our draft as best as we can, our true voice will appear. Because regardless of what happens, the passions we write about are still there.

17: BOULDERS

June, Keizer, OR: I was out of sync. Completely, one hundred percent not in flow with my writing. And because this is an honest book and hopefully a helpful one, the story belongs here. It didn't happen all at once, but was a gradual shift. But the reality of it didn't hit until things stopped working.

It went something like this. All was going well with my writing, and that was exciting. This book was evolving all on its own. Coincidences were plentiful, with meaningful messages that inspired my mind and guided my work. Then I started *pushing* it, for whatever reason.

It had to do with pages. I was aware that I often wrote many pages quickly and smoothly when in flow. It was easy when there, and felt more like sharing discoveries or adventures with friends than coming up with right words.

Then something changed. I started focusing on how many pages I had written, instead of the feeling behind them. Or why my speed was at times fast or slow. And during these couple of unpleasant weeks, I went from loving what I was doing to hardly liking it at all. But then the big U stepped in. "Garden" coincidences started up again that I knew were meant for me. But I still didn't know their meanings.

Before getting into that I'd like to share a point. I am not a gardener. Though I love looking at flowers and plants and decorating with them too, I don't enjoy working with them, digging in the dirt and all. But my husband does, which works out well.

I do love, however, having colorful foliage around and always make sure I do, in the house, on the deck, and in the yard. Eric ends up doing the yard work, and I help with its design, which seems to suit us both. But it's not a special interest that I think that much about, consciously anyway.

So the garden theme coming up again was surprising. There had been those other incidents with it too, that I have described. And when I realized my writing was off, a new cluster started again for some reason that I really wanted to know. The new pay-attention-here coincidences were these:

A description of a garden meditation. This might not sound like much of anything, but its inclusion in the book I was reading on a totally different subject felt out of place. Of course there are many possible images for use in meditation. But this one, where I found it and when, was strange, and certainly managed to catch my attention.

A book on symbols. Okay, what was striking here was not that gardens were included in the book, but *how* I found their place. After the meditation incident, I decided to look up their symbolism in a reference work I own. When I took the book from the shelf the pages fell open to—you guessed it—the section I was after: symbolism of gardens and flowers.

A book of quotations. I was paying close attention now. After what had just happened, I thought to look in another book, this time one of quotes. I had no reason why; it just felt right to do. When I randomly opened the book the same thing happened again, landing on some pages of garden quotes. I wasn't sure what to make of that!

And what did I end up with after all these garden incidents? At first nothing more than confusion. Beyond feeling that they were answers, nothing else was clear. I knew I was off with my writing, out of balance there for sure, and wanted back into its easy flow. But there seemed to be something I needed to do, or figure out or whatever, before that happened. So I decided to wait it all out, stop thinking of it and stop writing too, to wait and watch and see. And it didn't take long when I did until something stood out.

Strangely enough it was just a few plants in the yard. "Full-sun" plants that is, that really weren't what that said. They'd done beautifully in pots in half-sunny spots at previous houses, so I brought them along when we moved in here. But this house faces south, and our summers can be hot, and they didn't do well at all in those recommended full-sun places.

Then we visited a park with some gorgeous gardens and an open greenhouse, where a jungle of vibrant flowers lived, including some the same as my full-sun plants—in pots and in the shade! I couldn't believe it. No wonder mine had balked and been burned by the sun. Those locations suggested by others were not what they really needed, or where they grew their best and wanted to be.

And then it became pretty obvious, these metaphors of gardens as they pertained to my writing. Gardens and plants/creativity and growth—oh come on, why hadn't I seen it before? The images were repeatedly offered as symbols of these things. And why did the incidents begin *before* my trouble?

It's likely that the direction I was headed was obvious to the big U, but not me, that is. And so the signs and clues were provided to help. I'm glad I caught on quickly to the detour I had taken; it maybe was a lesson for us both. When it comes to our work, our mindset should feel good, and inspire us to write what we like. If it doesn't then something's off, and it helps to just stop, and feel our way back to that place, segueing into exploring some blocks we may meet on our way.

We're not always in flow. Even when we choose smooth waters to travel toward our goal, there will be boulders and rapids to encounter. How we navigate these spots will determine the pleasure and ease of our ride. Yet each of us must find our own way downstream.

I was reminded of this recently on an outing. Eric and I had stopped at a viewpoint along the Calapooia ("cal-a-poo-ya" if you're curious) near the tiny town of Brownsville. It was a spectacular setting. There, water tumbled over stone beds or meandered around them, in one special place. There were small, sparkly waterfalls and shiny glass pools. There were dozens of channels, all with water flowing through them in different directions, yet ending up in the same still pond below.

And that reminded me of our work. As writers we may share the same goal of writing with spirit, but that's where the similarity ends. Each of us must travel the distance of our personal channels to reach that special place, in spite of the boulders and rapids we encounter in the stream.

I think of these elements as the things that impede our flow, restrict or obstruct our writing space. But like water in the stream, we can change our speed, or go over or around these boulders, instead of being blocked, and get back in the current toward our goal where coincidence is our compass.

So that will always be our first step when blocked: re-finding flow. But until we do, there are some simple things we can do to start moving. Most of the blocks we may run up against are mental, but a few are physical, so let's talk about them first.

Life

The non-writing parts of our life affect our work. This is pretty self-evident; we all know what problems and obligations can do. Though ideas for harmonizing all parts of our lives are spread throughout the book, it may be helpful to repeat a few of these here. Everyday life can be tough at times.

One of the biggest boulders we face is often lack of time. We yearn to write, but are busy people. Some of us hold jobs or own businesses; all of us have stuff we must do besides work on our writing. Plus all the other things we *want* to do that take up time as well.

A good strategy here is acceptance, doing what we need to do outside of our work while keeping it still in mind. Making notes on ideas and insights, and writing when we can. Keeping our inspiration alive until we can really work again. Even a few sentences or paragraphs jotted down throughout the day can do this.

In my own case, I try to write something every day. When time is scarce, that may just be a sentence or two. Sometimes it's ideas; a new slant or subtopic, or the expansion of what's already written. This works well to keep things moving, if only just a little, and my mind where it needs to be, until I can once more write as freely as I want.

Problems are harder. It's difficult to focus and write as we wish with troubles going on. But lowering our standards for a bit can help. As a forgotten bookmark I just found suggests, take your best shot, and that's good advice for us here. Expecting less of ourselves during troubled times is wise. We can choose to simply do the very best we can, and that will keep us on track.

Fatigue

Tiredness can zap our writing. Low levels of energy can slow or even stop our work. Naturally we are all tired at times, but what

I'm talking about here are the effects that may occur from constant fatigue. This can be physical or mental, and both are detrimental. But both may respond to some coping techniques. Being tired can be a temporary slow-down if we know its cause.

As I've mentioned before, I sometimes have insomnia. When I do, I may go days with just a few hours sleep each night. This plays havoc on my writing, and other things as well, as it's a big effort to do most anything. But recently I came up with something that greatly helps the problem, that I can't believe I didn't see before: naps.

I know, I know; pretty common knowledge, but bear with me on this. I was taking naps all along, but not the right kind. With all that I wanted to do with my daytime, I was taking numerous *tiny* naps of five or ten minutes on insomnia days, which only helped a little bit.

Then I experimented, and tried an as-long-as-I-need-to-rest nap, and voila—much better. I could now enjoy the day after a really bad night's sleep and do my writing too, after one good, longer nap. And I'm happy with that for now, with plans for more experiments to improve upon it, and sleep more normal hours each night.

So the point for us as writers with regard to fatigue is to figure it out, to determine the cause of what's making us tired. And then to try stuff, experiment with different strategies, until we find one that works. Then get on with our writing when we can.

Boredom

Boring, dull, tedious. We all know that weary state these words describe, and can come up against it in our writing. How can this be when we write with deep feeling, sharing those things we care most about? It doesn't seem logical, but it happens, and we need to be aware of that, then do what needs doing to go around the block.

So what makes something boring anyway? Too much repetition or inaction. When things lack variety or interest or liveliness for too long of a time they become boring. They feel tedious and dull, and end up making us lethargic or simply tired.

Our thresholds for this are different. Some of us are comfortable with a lot more routine than others. It's a personal feel-good thing; a particular level of change and variety we crave. And when we're aware of this level, our writing will stir us, most of the time.

But not every minute. Like most anything enjoyable, we will like certain aspects of it better than others. Not every part of our writing will be fun. There will be parts of the process that will feel just okay—on a good writing day! But when we know our own mind and attention span these aspects will be relatively small, and our overall experience will be pleasant.

Our writing itself involves a variety of activities. To begin with, some topics or types of books require research. Then there's planning, plotting, or similar imagination work leading to some kind of outline or form. Finally, after a first draft is written, there's editing and rewriting, leading to a final polished story. Some of these tasks are bound to be more pleasurable to us than others.

I know for me, research is tops: my most favorite (very, very!) part of writing. And it comes most easily for me too. I am ever happy exploring my topic for frequent long stretches. I also love the rewrite; the polishing of words and ideas to make them shine. But the first writing of these words is an entirely different thing that can sometimes bog me down, and become boring too.

Then how can we cope with boredom? What can we do to feel eager and inspired again? In a few words: take a break from our writing. Get away from all work a while, as long as it takes. Do something physical or repetitive to give our minds a rest—our conscious minds anyway. Or at least back off from the part of our writing that's giving us trouble.

In addition to that we can work on the best parts of our story every time we write. Who says we need to write in a particular order? We certainly don't; there are no definite rules! We can write about what draws us most every single time. This will keep our work lively and interesting and just plain fun to do, while allowing big U guidance to come through.

Impatience

July, Keizer, OR: I was back on track. Things had gotten out of kilter for a little while, especially with my writing. But I'd been able to turn it around, and was back where I wanted to go, plus I was making some progress with impatience, perhaps my biggest boulder.

So thinking about that challenge right before sleep, my thoughts segued into: who am I now, and what is my main role in life? And the answer came quickly: an explorer who writes. I thought about that a bit, feeling its truth, then fell asleep. A little while later I awoke from a clear and clarifying dream.

The setting was a mall of sorts with lots of little shops. I seemed to be working for two of them, or rather trying to work for them between episodes of racing back and forth from one store to the other. This was no good, as they were left open, and unattended each time I was gone—but that was what was going on. Then in the middle of all the hurrying I made a discovery.

My purse was missing. I did the usual frantic search that did not help—it just wasn't there—along with the stream of worried thoughts, then quickly started planning what I needed to do. At that point the dream seemed complete and I woke up.

Lying there thinking about it, I understood its double meaning; personal for me, and public for us here. Its symbols of a purse as my identity and work defined by others were glaringly clear, along with its overall message. Impatience doesn't work. When we hurry and push our writing to meet some others' pace, we lose it heartfelt flow, along with ourselves, our sharing and passionate roles. And what a loss that is for us both and our readers!

Oftentimes impatience has nothing to do with the standards of others. Being in flow and connecting with the force feels wonderful, and makes our writing a joy. During quiet periods we may try to hurry on to the next exciting insight or message, instead of experiencing more subtle ones.

This doesn't work at all, because the direction and speed of the stream isn't our doing, only whether to join its flow. When we're calm these quieter times can be just as satisfying with their simple signs and revelations. Often, it seems, a cluster of incidents on the same theme will occur. But we've got to be patient to notice them to begin with, to benefit from their help.

I have a tough time with this. New possibilities are always exciting to me, and I love it when they appear. Colorful coincidence is really my thing. Discovery and surprise are fun, for the most part anyway, and often insightful. But when signs are more subtle, I may miss them entirely, until they repeat once again.

Skepticism can also lead to impatience with our writing. If we doubt synchronicity we want "proof," and are in a hurry to find it. Though blind, unexamined belief isn't wise, we do need to be open to the role that coincidence can play, then patient enough to watch it unfold. This also can be tough, and a block to our goal, when we're aiming to write what we feel. But there are steps we can take to get back on our writing path.

What helps is to recognize that we're impatient, and decide not to be. This really isn't as contradictory as it sounds. By noticing what we're doing and how it isn't working, we can decide to slow down. Then when things start moving with the help of higher wisdom, we'll find our right pace.

Procrastination

Another block we may face with our writing is procrastination; postponing or putting off what we most *want* to do. What? That doesn't even make sense! Why would we hold off from doing what inspires us the most? That's a confusing question for sure. Though the reasons for each of us may be complicated, here are some common ones often in play when we choose to delay our writing.

We are not ready. We're a little tired or tense or distracted or whatever, so not quite in the mood, and wonder if we should even try. How can we do a good job, after all, if we're not at our best?

Things aren't ready. It's not the best time; there is stuff going on with people and life. It's not the worst time, but not being ideal, should we even try? How can we write well when things aren't up to par?

It's too hard. Writing by itself is difficult. Writing to share our passion is harder yet. Should we even attempt to work when it feels so arduous? How can we write what we feel when it seems so hard?

It's too scary. The whole deal is just too daunting. Our story is too big or we'll sound like a dope or readers won't like what we say, or 101 other scenarios. How can we share what we care about when it's just too frightening? Should we even try it?

In one way or another, all our reasons for putting off writing have to do with fear. We're afraid it will end up unpleasant somehow. Instead of just starting, and going with the flow of insights and ideas, we try to anticipate ahead, negatively no less. It's an odd process, one we've probably all pursued, that takes us away from our goal, and away from the help of the Universe too.

When we procrastinate, other things suddenly seem important to do. It doesn't seem to matter what they are, we think, as long as we don't have to write! The whole thing is a little crazy, and often the best way out of our dilemma is to play a little trick on ourselves, a trick that will ease us right back where we really want to be: in the middle of our writing.

Here's how I do it. When I find myself putting off my writing, I allow myself some time to get *ready* to write. For me, this usually involves sharpening pencils, getting coffee, and choosing a spot to work, whether at home or at the library. I don't hurry with any of this, just take my time doing some things that ease me into the mood and lead up to my writing. Following that, I read over some of what I wrote last—a paragraph or a page—for as long as that feels right, and then write a brand new sentence.

This usually is effective. As I finish writing that fresh new phrase and putting it onto the page, a little thrill runs through me. In that instant things change. My work feels fun again, and I'm eager to get on with it, and ready to be inspired by coincidence as I go. Getting back into flow is often that simple.

Confusion

The last common blockage that comes to mind is confusion. We may be unclear about our work at any point of the project. This may be about our subject or story or structure or plot, or any aspect of these elements. Or about the thoughts and ideas we're planning to share. There really are unlimited numbers of details that can confuse us, if we let them, about the work we're trying to do.

The answer again is to go with the flow around these blocking stones; let the Universe provide the pull to where we want to go. There are a couple of things that we can do to help ourselves along while we get back to that moving place.

We can adjust our plan. If we have set up a simple outline, how is it working? Is it effective as a map of our route? Or does it seem like it needs to be changed in some way? Sometimes we need to add material to our writing plan. And sometimes we need to eliminate the same.

We can go by the feel. If our outline is brief, made up of a few words or phrases for each section of our story, does it feel like enough? Or is it confusing to know what direction to go? Alternately, if our outline is detailed, does it feel like too much? And confusing to figure out how to cover it all? A plan that's helpful yet comfortable will work best.

I have experienced both extremes. Because I love to research, I may investigate more sources in more depth than I need, and take too many notes, then spend lots of extra time sorting through them. This makes it confusing to find what's really relevant for my writing. The same thing applies to my outlines. When they are too involved, there seems too much to cover. I start feeling overwhelmed and confused until I greatly pare them down.

I've gone the other way as well. Pushing toward briefness, I've taken it too far, ending up with a useless plan. For me anyway, one or two words describing a segment are just not enough. But a couple of phrases describing the same are perfect, and I've learned to find my balance there.

Our outlines will be tentative, as the big U lends a hand, with coincidental guiding signs about our plan. And we will notice them and understand them and benefit from them too, if we feel clear instead of confused.

18: REWRITING

Once the first draft of your book is finished, congrats to you! What a special thing that is, for the hardest part of writing your heartfelt story is done. I like to take some kind of break at this point to celebrate, and maybe you will too. It's unusual to have gone from wanting to write to have actually carried it through!

Our first drafts need to be proofread for incorrect spelling, punctuation, and grammar. If you're skilled in these you may choose to do it yourself. Most writers, though, hire an editor to do this as well as correct other manuscript errors before their book is published.

What we'll explore here is more of a polishing really; a final refinement of what we have written. A final going-over our words to make sure they shine. A rewriting of our work in whatever way leaves it better than before. This is challenging but fun. We have the finished first draft to work from to enhance and clarify, to rework so our feelings come through. And polishing it to do so is usually not a hard thing.

It's a matter of listening to our voices through the stories we have written. How do they sound when we read them aloud? Do their words sound like us, like the way that we talk and the way that we think too? Writing in *your* natural language will sound natural because it is, instead of stilted or forced.

Another thing to consider when rewriting is necessity. Do parts of our writing include non-essential words? If so, they muddy up our meanings and detract from the rhythm of our prose. Rereading will help us spot these sections, and decide what's important to keep. A drama unfolding this morning reminded me of this point.

A hurricane was approaching Florida, where several of our relatives live in the city of Jacksonville. It was a big one, with furious winds and high storm surges. And our nephew lives by the water. His home's on the St. James River that flows into the sea, so those surges are a danger, especially when predicted to be deep and wide. So when a storm approaches there is always the need to decide what to do.

Here's where the essential information comes in. With a hurricane like this, there's often advice to get out, to evacuate the area. But that isn't always the best thing. Sometimes gridlocked roads and fearful drivers pose more of a threat than the storm. But it depends on many factors about the particular storm that is on its way.

So our nephew sifted through the data—the important stuff that's known—and then decided what to do, while ignoring all the other bits that added nothing. And if you're curious, they all stayed at his mother's, which was further from the water, and waited the hurricane out.

Then back to our topic here. We need to keep what's essential in our writing, and drop the rest, based on what's important. Doing this will help us write in a smooth and natural manner. So that with a little polishing, our stories end up as intended, full of personal passion and easy to read.

19: WRITING—BY COINCIDENCE

I've experienced three simple steps for writing in the flow of coincidence. We've explored them in various ways in this book. Here, I'd like to summarize them a bit, while seeing where that will go. For as usual when I write with focus and feeling, the big U is there too, with helpful messages and clues. And I'm excited to see what these may be!

Focus on what you want.

As writers, we need to focus on our intentions; what our goal is for our work. We can do this before or while we write. This can be a simple thing to do. Just a few minutes going over what we now want to say is usually enough, and will send out a signal for help as needed.

This can be about anything related to our work, whether the writing itself or something else. The important thing is the centering on intent. So we may focus on a description, conversation, mood, or whatever we want to write, while being open for insights and signs.

For instance, during the writing of my first book I had some eerie events involving old letters that I have mentioned here. So when I told these stories, I wanted to convey a sentimental mood, for once I'd solved the mystery of my connection with those letters, I'd felt a link through time with their authors too. And I wanted to share that sense—that gift from the past—with my readers.

So I focused on that, thinking about it from time to time as I got busy writing up the story. And as I did, I was drawn to certain letters in the group, and parts of these in particular. Then it felt right to put together a composite sort of example, sharing bits of the thoughts and feelings of the people. This worked well. The sentiments and personal nature of the authors came through, and my writing was easy and smooth. The focus kept me on track and triggered the helpful flow.

Feel your energy

I find that the second step of writing in flow is to feel your energy. Be aware of the tone of what you perceive. This will be both inner intuitions and outer events as well. Your sense that something is personally significant will enable you to recognize meaningful coincidence and use it to write your very best.

Something we might remember is how the intensity of these can vary. Synchronicities can stop us in our tracks with their amazing tricks. We feel awed to receive such magical messages. And it's easy to understand their messages when we do. Flowing with these is easy because we have no doubts about the intensity of our feelings or the next step we're inspired to take.

But coincidence is often more subtle. An incident occurs that feels a little like something, but of what we're not sure. Still, we sense that it's more than a fluke; that it's meant as a sign for us. We can wait awhile and refocus; that's often enough, and the big U will take it from there with additional guiding signs that we are then able to use in or writing.

These subtle nudges aren't necessarily about small things. Sometimes we are just not as perceptive as usual. So a slight significance may be all that we feel. Then too, the Universe knows the best sign for us at any particular time, and that may be a subtle one.

Trust your own feelings about coincidence. What has meaning for you may not for anyone else. Sometimes if you share, others may say, "Wow!" or maybe "Cool," or maybe "Huh? I don't get it." But then they don't need to. As long as an event is meaningful to you, that is all that matters. For each of your synchronicities is about you, and others experience their own.

For example, once while writing *The Secret Language of Synchronicity*, I was thinking about writer's voice. We went out for lunch, and my dessert cookie's fortune read, "Use soft words and hard arguments." When I read that I got goose-bumps; for the connection to my thoughts was so clear. Then Eric read it and said, "Cool!" as the link was obvious for him too.

However, when we saw something unusual a few days ago, it was different; a symbol for me that meant nothing to him. It was surely one of those "Huh? I don't get it" kinds of signs. Here's what happened.

I was getting ready to start this chapter. As I went over my outline notes something didn't feel quite right: there were too many of them. And really, the whole book was on writing in flow, anyway. So instead of the current plan, it seemed something briefer was needed. And I'd have to start fresh with this part again. Those were the thoughts I was having as we headed out to do some shopping and such in town.

Right away we came to a fountain filled with suds. Some kids had added soap to the water, making a mess. Immediately the image brought the words "washed clean" to mind, as in a brand new chapter. Go ahead, do that, thumbs up, it confirmed to me. A summary of some points will work better than the plan you had before. To Eric though, it meant nothing more than a crazy amount of bubbles, which was fine, as the message was mine.

Follow your energy

The third important step of writing with the flow is to follow your energy; to go with what feels right or true, to take steps that bring you joy or the better path of two. Doing this is your link to higher wisdom and practical answers also, concerning your writing goals.

Try to do this with every part of your work. Follow your vibes regarding incidents that happen and the actual writing itself. Follow your urges about what you write and how you do it, as well as intuitions you're not sure will even apply. When you do, it will all come together in time, when your feelings are your guide.

As you write with meaning, give it your all; share your uniqueness with others. Your work will convey this deep point of view that your readers will sense. The following stories illustrate doing this, and not, respectively.

September, Salem, OR: I had met Sophie for coffee. She had just come back from an RV trip to Canada and Alaska, and was sharing some tales. I asked about meals; did they mostly make their own? Or did they eat local cuisine along the way? "We mostly made our own meals," she said, "shopping at grocery stores and eating pretty simple, mainly just cooking at night, with sandwiches and snacks like carrots and nuts during the day. But we did eat out a little, and had some delicious local meals. And then there was the thing with THE PIE."

That made me curious, so naturally I asked. Sophie went on, "One day, after we'd hiked on a lakeside trail, I felt like eating something sweet. So I said to Larry, 'Let's go have some pie at that little place in town that we saw yesterday. You know, the one with the sign saying pie was their thing.' He was all for it, so we washed up and drove on over.

"I ordered apple pie and Larry ordered strawberry-rhubarb.

And once we were there and saw all those delicious-looking pies, we wanted ours à la mode. So we asked, and they said yes, they could do that. But then when they brought our pie, the scoop of ice cream on top was only about as big as a silver dollar. We were so disappointed!"

I asked her how the pie tasted. "The pie itself was very good, even though it was on the small side. But we were shocked when they brought the bill. The total was triple the norm for those two pieces of pitiful pie à la mode!"

Later at home, I was thinking about Sophie's pie story. Of all her tales from the two months of travel through extraordinary country, this was what most stood out. It somehow felt relevant to deep writing, but I wasn't sure how. I told Eric about it, who replied, "I have a pie story too, which I don't think you've ever heard. It wasn't a big deal or anything, just a fun experience—way different than Sophie's."

"Tell me!" I said.

"It happened on my big bike trip before I met you. I had ridden the length of California, and across the states of Oregon and Idaho. One afternoon I had just crossed into Montana, pretty close to the town of my friends, but needed to stop and eat. And was tired of all the stuff I'd brought along. So when I saw a little place by the side of the road with a sign that read 'Fresh Pie,' I decided to make that lunch.

"The place was bustling. There were lots of people sitting around, mostly eating pieces of pie, plus others picking up racks of whole pies. It was obviously very popular, and I was anxious to try their specialty. I found a seat and then ordered—apple pie à la mode.

"When it came I wasn't disappointed. The piece was huge—about a sixth of an entire pie. And on top was a big scoop of ice cream to set it off. And man, was it delicious! I remember thinking it was the best apple pie à la mode ever. And after I ate and the bill came, it was a bargain too!"

Wow, what a difference between the two restaurants. Both were founded by someone creative, of that I felt sure; someone who likely loved baking, which had resulted in the creation of some very special pies. But there the similarities ended. While Eric's pie place was generous with its offerings, Sophie's place was not, being miserly instead.

And both of them valued their creations, and were probably proud of them too, as was right for them to be, plus chose to share them with others. But the baker of Eric's pie place gave it all that she or he had, while Sophie's seemed to hold back. As though thinking, here, enjoy what I have specially made, but don't take too much. And with these musings on yummy pie I understood the link to our writing, and am inspired to share my take on it here.

When we write with deep feeling we share what we care about through our creation of words. And then we offer that specialty to others. When we do this, we need to give freely, be open-hearted throughout, because that generosity is enjoyable for both us and our readers.

And then a little footnote: a short while after working on this section, I was at St. Vinny's looking at some books. One had a fun introduction about the author chef, whose love of cooking had become a passion. Exactly. Anyone for pie?

And finally, step out with courage to follow the flow of coincidence as you write, knowing it's the start of a grand adventure. It is exciting to be part of the brave ones in line for the ride.

Today, Corrales, NM: Nancy sent me an email and mentioned that the big hot air balloon festival began tomorrow, but that there were already fifty or sixty colorful balloons floating over

her house. I thought about these symbols that still finely stand
for writing and sharing our words to me, and those eager
balloonists, so keen to start their ride. Then the insight came that
this is really our very last step to our adventuresome goal. Write
what's exciting, get in the basket, and drop the rope. Then float
where the winds of coincidence blow.

And a fun, for-the-moment finale: I had written up the balloon
incident, thinking that would probably be the last coincidence
story in this book, but you know how that goes. Do stories ever
really end? Not our own stories anyway, when synchronicity
plays a part. The following clusters of clues are still occurring,
and I am collecting them here. I have a feeling their message
may be surprising to all of us.

Over these same few days I had been thinking about a note
from my son written many years before. The letter itself was part
of a coincidence I hadn't yet shared. And I'd been thinking about
it, that maybe I should do so, as the book was nearly done. But
there really wasn't an appropriate place. Here's how I re-
discovered the note.

It was January, and I was thinking of writing this second book
on coincidence. So much had happened during my first book's
writing that I thought one on that topic would be good. But how
much experience did I have on the subject, anyway? And was
what I'd learned right for the idea?

In the middle of these thoughts I got the urge to reorganize a
cabinet, which was home to a wealth of book-related things.
There were notebooks and journals and miscellaneous papers of
writing and research I'd done, plus lists of ideas and thoughts on
the same. And in a thin folder, mixed in with these, something
quite different: a note from Jason, my son.

I didn't know why it was in that folder, mixed in with very
different stuff; in fact I barely remembered the note at all. And
when I reread it, and saw what it was about, I was more

surprised still, for it concerned coincidence, and was itself a coincidence, to find it then, and carried a most encouraging message for me. Here's what Jason had written, back when he worked in a movie theater:

September, Monterey, CA: "Hi, Mom—I just wanted to tell you about a synchronicity incident that happened tonight at work. I went in to screen two where {movie name} was showing, after the movie had ended, to check out the auditorium before the next show. There was a woman sitting alone in the theater. I began to straighten up, and to be friendly asked her what she thought of the film. This is what she said:

"'It was wonderful! I could see that movie again and again!'

"'It really makes you think, huh?' I commented. She agreed. Then I said, 'I've been trying to get my mom to come see it, because the topic is what she studies.' She then asked about your interests and told me about herself. She is a therapist, and soon will be teaching at MPC about the mind power dimension, and is writing her thesis on coincidence. She gave me her card for you, in case you'd like to talk or read her dissertation. Pretty cool, huh?"

There was a date jotted in the margin that I'd added at the time, which oddly was over twenty years before. I had no concept, consciously at least, that I'd been studying my subject for so long! Metaphysics, yes; I'd read my first book on the mysterious powers of mankind when I was just nine or ten, and kept reading and even experimenting myself.

A little friend and I were the only kids on the block that often played with ESP instead of toys. But my knowledge of synchronicity and passion for it had begun as an adult, far earlier than I remembered. But the big U reminded me that, hey, you've explored these gifts for a long, long, while. And sharing what you've learned is what's right for you.

But there was more to come. I had taken out that note from

him that I'd found those months before, about coincidence and the theatre. A theatre that was wisely named "The Dream." Then an email came from Jason with an old picture attached—of him at the very same place!

Let me tell you about the Dream. It was a small movie theatre in Monterey, California, near the edge of the sea. Eclectic in an exotic sort of way, it was beautiful and hip. The elaborate "Dream" sign looked like a Tiffany mosaic of colorful glass. The interior looked ritzy and rich. Dark woods and carved botanicals added to the feel.

The Dream was unique. Luxuries such as double seat booths and three curtained screens were private and special. The ceiling was soft-lit and changed hues as the music began. The mood felt as fun and exciting as the movie you came to see. And people loved it, being so different from anyplace else. And the movies aimed to please as well. There were traditional films and artsy films and other oddball favorites, shown week after week to regulars.

The picture Jason sent was of him presenting the intro to one of these popular films. He was enjoying himself; it was clear from the scene. And from what he has told me, everyone who came to watch did too. So his fond memories of those times are of friendship and fun.

Then there's the symbolism of the theater's name. If a dream's an aspiration, and a movie's a story, then the theatre's what holds the two, or what contains the pleasant vision between its walls, while our book holds our vision between its covers, and conveys its story through our words.

So the bottom line for us here with these theatrical prompts is to remember our earliest dreams. Those visions and yearnings are the stuff of our passions. There may be some symbols and signs to make sure we never forget these pleasant visions.

And here's a postscript. Remembering the Dream Theatre

(now gone), and adventures when living in Monterey was so fun that I decided to check out a book on movie theatre history. There was only one available, *Ticket to Paradise: American Movie Theaters and How We Had Fun*, by John Margolies and Emily Gwathmay, at Salem Library.

The book was beautiful, with a profusion of historic photos of magnificent old theatres and accompanying text. Including a small one, coincidentally, from my home town. To get an idea of how odd this is, consider this: I grew up in Grants Pass, a small town encircled by mountains in southern Oregon. The population was around 10,000 back then, and there were two movie houses, plus a drive-in show, period.

Stranger yet is that from thousands of US theatres, the Rogue made it into the book, because it really wasn't that special. But its marquee had a deco look, and that's what the picture was, along with a thought about movies and small-town kids.

Then the insight came about my own mental dream theatre, where I've been seeing stories ever since that young age. Have you? Those old dreams are apt to be a part of your passions still, and the stories you ultimately will tell. What are your dreams?

So we've explored the three steps for writing in flow as focus, feel, and follow. Here are a few ideas to keep that simple and smooth. When you're authentic, detailed, and clear with your words, your passionate voice will come through.

Be Authentic

Be O-D-D; be you. Odd? As in strange or peculiar? What does that have to do with our writing? A great deal more than you might think. But first, let's clarify what I mean by that term "O-D-D."

It's a personal distinction. In my family "odd" is used in another way, as a fun and flattering term. We think of it as a badge of distinction, of being authentically ourselves. So someone who is O-D-D is original and unique, unlike any other, the only one of their kind. And that's a good thing. It's been that way for quite a while, and is a great way to think. And a little three-year-old taught us the lesson.

Here's the story. When my niece was young, my sister sewed many of her clothes. Gayle was good and creative, often changing parts of patterns and designs to make some special pieces. One outfit though, that should have been cute, did not turn out as planned.

It was a sort of jumpsuit for tykes. When it was done, Gayle tried it on Karen, and then had to stifle a laugh. The whole thing looked just plain strange, and not even close to what she'd envisioned. But Gayle knew she could always rethink and redo the outfit.

Karen loved it though, especially some ribbon trim that stuck out instead of laying flat, as intended, and didn't want her mom to change a thing. And she was very excited to show her grandma besides. So Gayle left it alone and later told her mom that yes, she had made the suit. But that it had turned out, well— and here she spelled it out—sort of O-D-D.

And then that stuck. The word in our group segued into meaning something or someone different, in a remarkable way. Someone unusual who knew what they liked and did it. Someone authentic then, and brave. So be O-D-D whenever you can. Remember what makes you tick and go there. When you share your difference in your writing, your readers will feel it.

June, Salem, OR: My friend Jane and I had met for coffee at a busy café. It was fun, nibbling on cookies, sharing the news, plus some stories from our pasts. There were always plenty of incidents it seemed to share. She told me a couple of cute ones about some preteen kids; happy boys full of life and natural joy.

These stories stayed with me. They weren't complex or anything, just simple accounts of lighthearted kids out to enjoy their day. But somehow they felt like something more. So I made a note to keep them handy, for whatever else might come that might have to do with our writing subject here. And that's what happened. But before getting into the rest of that, here are the stories, as told to me by Jane.

August, Berkeley, CA: "At the time this happened I worked in a bookstore. Some of my favorite customers were preteen boys who were so full of life and joy. I liked to chat with these young guys, to hear their happy adventures. One day a group of three came into the store. I greeted them then asked, 'What have you boys been up to today?' One of them stepped forward to answer.

"'Well,' he said, 'first of all we all rode our bikes to the Cinnabon. And then we each ate a roll. Then we rode to a store to look for a certain book. But they didn't have it, so we decided to come here.' At this point the narrator looked around a bit bewildered and said, 'Where are we anyway?' All of us nearby enjoyed a good chuckle out of that."

Jane remembered another happy-go-lucky young guy. "Another time a boy was browsing in the store with his dad. They finished shopping, and brought some things up to the counter. As I was ringing up the gentleman's books, his son kept scooting his own selection, an adventure comic book, closer to me. He was obviously excited about owning it, and didn't want it left out. He was also eying some bookmarks on a nearby rack. His dad noticed and asked, 'Would you like to have a new bookmark too?'

"'Boy, would I!' the young man exclaimed, then after a minute added, 'This is just about the happiest day of my life!'"

A month or so later, while looking over my outline, I remembered the stories. Some notes about the relationship between good energy and writing in flow reminded me of the boys, for feeling what we like and following it is sometimes easier when we're young. I shared my thoughts with Eric, who told me a bicycling story he had forgotten to tell me before, an incident once more on the same thing: going with our joy.

July, Salem, OR: "I was riding west, toward the tiny town of Rickreal. A nice bike trail I was included in my route. It offered a 'dedicated bicycle rest stop' made up of a couple benches, a flag pole, and a plaque committed to a promoter of state trails. There was also a rusty old mailbox sitting on one end of a bench.

"I stopped to take a break, and noticed the flag on the mailbox was up. There were no houses nearby the stop at all. I was curious, so opened the box to take a look. Inside were a notebook and pen. People had written in the book—bicyclists that is—about their thoughts and rides for the day. It was interesting to read their comments and where they were from. One entry, simply printed, ended with the words, 'Honor the Turtle.'

"I had no idea what that was all about. So I kept reading the entries, where others were wondering the same thing. Then I came to an answer by the original poster. Turned out to be a bicyclist who was only ten years old, and joining in the fun. He seemed to love riding, and sharing, and something else: his toy animal named Mr. Turtle.

"I didn't know if Mr. Turtle came along on the rides, but got the feeling that he might. What really came through was the respect. It was obvious that this young boy felt his riding and his companion were important.

"Some other riders chimed in then, with endings of their own to honor Mr. Turtle, which must have made the kid, when he read it, really glad. Everyone who wrote there sounded happy to be doing what they liked to do. The book set down some feelings and stories that otherwise might not have been shared, and I added my own turtle tribute in honor of that."

As I began writing down these stories, a footnote appeared that echoed their message, to make sure I went ahead and included them here. And it's good it did, because I had been thinking that maybe they were too abstract to put at all.

As often happens, Deidre wrote me an email, with far more meaning than she knew.

She randomly sent me a quote from an inspiring collection that made up the book I had once given to her. The quote was about recognizing joy as a sign of our path. Now that's fun to know when we're being authentically ourselves.

Be Detailed

September, Keizer, OR: I was sitting on the couch, working on a different section of this chapter about writing in the flow of coincidence. Nearby, Eric was involved with his photography, sprawled out on the floor. Deciding that I needed a break, I asked how his project was going. "Pretty good," he said. "This new frame fits well, and moving the rose picture to that other spot on the wall will work better."

I thought about that a minute. "But it looked good in the old spot too," I said.

"Yeah, but you couldn't get close enough to see the sparkle of the dew."

Details. The particulars of the picture; the small parts most important to see. In this instance, dewdrops sparkling on a rose were an essential element of the image, and important to Eric too. And he knew that, and intuitively knew that the first high spot on the wall didn't work.

He'd tried to accept it for awhile. I'd seen him stand close to the wall and look up at the picture, then gaze at it from across the room. But in the end it just wasn't acceptable. So he moved it to a better place to do what he'd intended: highlight the sparkle of the color of a beautiful rose.

It is the same with our writing. Details share that sparkle, the specifics that are important to us, the parts we care most about. And they do this throughout our story. Without details, though, our writing can be shallow and dull. But with details woven in with our words, our stories light up with feeling.

What kind of details should we use? That will depend on us, on the things we find essential; the things we are passionate about. Particulars will carry the meaningful tones of our tales. These may be sensual or mental, inner or outer incidents or states; details that bring our readers close. Details that let them experience what we do.

As I wrote this book, my priority was coincidence, in particular those events about my writing. Though I included synchronicities about a few other things, those concerning work were most important to me. And so those messages that happened to occur as I was writing this book are what I needed to tell in detail.

"Needed to tell" puts it mildly. I'm crazy about the topic. So sometimes trying to share what I felt seemed impossible to do. But through the description of minutiae of what I'd sensed or seen, it was more likely to come through. This isn't infallible. Describing an experience, even in detail, isn't like living it. But when it's done well, it's the second best thing, and conveys to our readers our feelings down deep.

When I started writing in earnest, I wrote for a couple of sites. These were article collections, and authors could write what they wished. There was a small payment for each article upfront, plus a monthly bonus based on popularity of the piece.

I ended up with dozens of articles, most on interior design that included antiques. These were easy, being a couple of subjects I knew very well. But my heart wasn't in them. I was writing what interested others, but me not so much, and that wasn't too fun. Pretty soon there was no enjoyment at all, so I quit.

For a while. After a break I missed it. Not the writing I'd lately been doing, but some I'd done long before about very different things. Most of this was unpublished; personal journal entries and letters, but I loved that heartfelt sharing through words. And that's what I wanted to do again now with the articles.

Then I decided to do an experiment: write a piece about metaphysics, what I was interested in most, and see what happened. Some topic of it that was familiar to me. A topic I could have fun with, exploring with a tongue-in-cheek style. Astrology seemed a great fit, so I chose it. Though my beliefs about it weren't clear, its natal sign profile for Eric was good, and I knew I could write about that.

So I came up with my theme and a playful title, "How to Keep Your Taurus Man Heavenly Happy" and dug in. And wow, what a difference it made this time around! The writing itself was a breeze. The tone was light-hearted, but was of substance too, from years of a couple's experience. For I had learned and lived with my Taurus guy for quite a long while. And made sure to share my insights with readers through—you guessed it—details.

The details were chosen by feel. Those ideas that felt most significant had to go in. So, for example, in a section on the importance of touch to Taurus, I covered things such as linens, clothes, and even upholstery, then did the same for each sub-topic of the article, detailing both my experience and Eric's.

Along the way (it turned out to be a pretty long piece) there were a couple coincidences that offered more help, as they clarified thoughts and confirmed my direction. So I continued, ending up with a whimsical, but not, piece that was really fun to write. And I was happy with that.

Apparently my readers were too. The article was read at least ten times more than any of my others, day after day. The worth was in the details. Those particulars that felt important to me were able to touch others as well. And that's what we're after. But yes, there was that catchy title too. Which, by the way, still appears on the Internet here and there, as "heavenly happy this" and "heavenly happy that," though I removed all my articles when the articles program folded.

Be Clear

We can aim for conciseness with short words and phrases, those more often known and used. These usually have the benefit of sounding more rhythmic when read too. But when choosing our words, their meanings are what matters, and sometimes the shorter ones are not right. So choosing the best words to express our best thoughts is wise, whatever their length.

And then there are sentences. Conciseness here is often good for clarity. Too many ideas combined can be confusing. But too many short phrases can be repetitive and dull. Longer phrases are helpful to keep our writing fresh, so it's good to add some to our prose. And this happens pretty instinctively when we *listen* to our words.

What I'm talking about is the old adage to write like we speak. That is, I think, the best way to be clear. To be completely clear, through our own voice, our own words, our own unique way, each time we set out to write. For each of us then, the arrangement and simplicity of our words will vary based on the natural way we speak. And our readers will be most likely to understand what we mean. Your words will be clear when you write in your personal voice.

What's the best way to do this? As another helpful adage goes, by talking on paper. It works well to think of our readers as friends, which they often tend to become anyway, then imagine sitting down with a few to visit, and telling them our stories. Doing this removes our restraints, allowing our voice to come through, easy and clear.

20: GAMES

Okay, I didn't see this coming. There'd been some sleepless nights lately, as I was moving closer to my reserved slot for editing and formatting help. I was excited: this book was coming together, and I was rushed a bit too, because I still needed to finish writing plus all the typing too.

But I needed to stay in sync. Which meant being extra aware of prompts and ideas that popped into mind, and outer symbols and signs. Intuition would be there to guide me through, if I listened for it.

And so it was 2 a.m. on a Tuesday, and I was up on the couch with my first cup of a couple coffees for the day, and scribbling in a notebook about games. Here's why. I had been lying in bed awake, thinking and not sleeping, when the word "games" came to mind. As I'd been thinking about this writing, I then thought, what? Games and the book? What about games, anyway? Then in a flash I saw that I needed to break up the push to "The End." And that games made up in flow had prizes too.

So in the name of the, you know, game, I asked the next question: what kind of game should I play? Because I am not really a game person at all, in the traditional sense of premade board or card or electronic ones, that is. But mental games were a whole different deal, and had always been fun. So I'd go with the flow.

Here's what came up quickly. Tow coincidence games, spread over the rest of the day, for the benefit of the book and me. Game one: I would choose ten things that stood out from something I read. Game two: I would choose then things that caught my attention from something I saw, then do follow-up on each, to look for connections or messages about our work here.

My focus question would be: is there anything else I need to know about writing with the help of coincidence? Have I forgotten any important points? That was the plan, and I was curious to start. I thought I'd wait until morning though, to give my sleep another go, and hoped you'd play along.

The next morning I began the first game. I decided to use a dictionary, as I'd always liked them, being a word person and all. But besides that, it seemed the perfect source of most anything to read, as I chose an older encyclopedic one.

I began by setting the big thick book on the table. It was heavy and extensive, several thousand pages long. Then I thought about my question for a few minutes and what I was trying to do; play a game with coincidence about my writing, and be open for insights and clues, and consider anything I was drawn to in the book as a possible answer.

I thumbed through some pages at random, glancing at words I both knew and didn't, and reading their meanings. The first ten that attracted or made me curious were these, along with their meanings that I liked best.

1. Chime: spoken rhythmically; harmonious sound.
2. Drop letter: letter delivered from the identical post office where it is posted.
3. Echo: repetition of certain sounds, as in poetry.
4. Emollient: soothing and softening.
5. Formulus: an assistant, as to a magician or scholar.

6. Gamut: entire range of something.
7. Hieroglyphics: symbols having hidden meanings.
8. High-spirited: Being courageous with a fiery spirit.
9. Realm: the scope of any influence or power.
10. Muse: a goddess inspiring arts and learning.

Later in the day I was out, so went ahead with game two in a Salvation Army store. The ten items that attracted me were these.

1. A pair of large needlework pictures of peacocks.
2. A quote on a picture about each person being a unique expression of the Cosmos.
3. A certificate from a star-naming registry.
4. A watercolor scene of a 1900s picnic, with children releasing a butterfly kite.
5. A little girl, browsing, costumed in sheer, purple butterfly wings.
6. A journal with a fortune cookie design, and two prominent fortunes about letting creativity soar, and following your dreams.
7. A shiny green-glass-covered dish shaped like a shamrock.
8. A broken gambling wheel with numbers and some kind of game.
9. A package of fifty different colored spools of thread.
10. A leather covered bottle marked "Curacao," with designs of a turtle, macaw bird, and a tropical scene.

Back home, I went over the word list, looking for similarities or connections. What I noticed first was that "chime" and "echo" both referred to the pleasant sound of words, and that the meaning of "emollient" could be in a sense too. Two words, "formulas" and "hieroglyphics," had a reference to magic or mystery, and another pair, "drop letter" and "muse," to writing and the arts. Then "realm" and "gamut" to the range of things, and "high-spirited" to courage.

Then I looked at the second list of attention-grabbing things, again checking for similarities or connections. Interestingly, six of the ten items had to do with the concepts of courage and creativity in some form or another, with my personal connotations: the butterfly kite picture, the girl with butterfly wings, the fortune cookie journal, the picture with a quote about individual uniqueness, and the pictures of the peacocks.

Another couple had to do with luck: the gambling game wheel and the shamrock dish. The last item, the leather-decorated bottle brought up nothing; it was just creative and very well done. Aha! Another to add to the creativity and courage category. Oh, and about the shamrock-shaped dish: I have a four-leaf clover on the cover of *The Secret Language of Synchronicity*, so there's that. A good luck symbol in several ways, about several things to me.

So what did we end up with then from this, other than some made up games? A message about creative courage, for sure. An encouragement to write our stories in our unique voices that sound smooth and rhythmic to our ears. Then to let go and release them to the stars, to be part of the mystery realms, for the muse of coincidence is always on our side!

21: THE FINAL WORDS

We've reached the end of this story, our tale of writing with passion through help of coincidence. I'd like to leave you now with a few final thoughts.

It's Genuine.
The guidance of the Universe is real, and ready to help. You can have fun exploring it—in your life and your work.

It's Mysterious.
The mechanics of coincidence are a mystery, and always will be. But you can learn to flow with its conjuring tricks.

October, Keizer, OR: This book was nearly finished. I was typing up the last bit, except these final few pages that weren't written yet, for I had a feeling there was something to come, and didn't want to miss it.

Then our neighbor came over. In his hands were a couple of orchids. He'd found the tossed plants, he said, and would we like one? "Sure," I answered, "we'll take it," and was glad for the gift of the flower; a flower of mystery and flair I knew little about.

I did have my own impressions of the flowers though. Orchids were symbols to me of mystery, of exotic and delicate beauty, that thrived in areas of warmth and mist. And of strangely unique characteristics too.

I'd heard a bit about "ghost orchids" that were rare and hard to find, and grew in only a few lush spots. The flowers of these beauties seemed to float in the air, it was said, and were nearly transparent in low light as they hovered as mysterious white ghosts.

I wanted to raise the flower. Arriving when it did as a happenchance gift felt meaningful. Then that plant that meant "mystery" to me seemed to stand for the mystery of coincidence too. And I was grateful for that gift from the big U.

I needed to do some research of the requirements of the plant, to enable it to be happy and grow. But before I could do that I needed a new pot. The plant's roots were bare and all our other flowerpots were full.

So I called Eric, who had gone down to the closest Goodwill to look around. He was just leaving the store when I did. "I'll go back in and take a look at their pots," he said. "How big should it be?"

"About five or six inches tall would be good, and with a drain hole in the bottom."

"Okay." Then after a minute or two, "How about an *orchid pot*?"

"What?"

"An orchid pot. There is a five-inch ceramic pot right here that's labeled as that on the bottom, with ventilation holes in the sides."

"That's our pot!" I said.

Somehow I knew that mystery gift was meant to do well.

It's always there.

The help of the Universe is there for us whenever we need it, each time we choose to ask, through our focus and our dreams. May your incidents be full of meaning, as you write—and flow—with coincidence!

Thank you for taking the time to read *Writing—by Coincidence*. If you enjoyed it, please think about telling your friends, or posting a brief review. I would appreciate it; word of mouth really is an author's best friend!

All the best, Jenna

REFERENCES

Burham, Sophie. *A Book of Angels: Reflections on Angels Past and Present and True Stories of How They Touch our Lives.* New York: Ballantine Books, 1990.

Christopher, Thomas. *In Search of Lost Roses.* New York, New York: Summit Books, 1989.

Eco, Umberto. *Confessions of a Young Novelist.* Cambridge, Mass.: Harvard University Press, 2011.

George, Rana. *The Essential Lenormand: Your Guide to Precise & Practical Fortunetelling.* Woodbury, MN: Llewellyn Publications, 2014.

Gigerenzer, Gerd. *Gut Feelings: The Intelligence of the Unconscious.* New York: Viking, 2007.

Gilbert, Elizabeth. *Big Magic: Creative Living Beyond Fear.* New York: Riverhead Books, 2015.

Margolis, John & Gwathmay, Emily. *Ticket to Paradise: American Movie Theaters and How We Had Fun.* Boston: Little, Brown and Company, 1991.

Rogers, Randolph J. *The Key of Life: A Metaphysical Investigation.* Bloomington, Indiana: Transformation Media

Books, USA, 2009.

Russell, Caroline, editor. *Climbing Roses*. West Huntspill, Somerset, Great Britain: Parsimony Press, 2000.

ABOUT THE AUTHOR

Jenna Moore Fuller, a former vintage books dealer, has studied metaphysics for many years, with a special interest in coincidence. She has written for websites and magazines, and kept longtime journals of her own synchronicities, along with those of family and friends.

After seeing the importance of words in coincidence, she focused on understanding its language and discovered the different styles through which the Universe seems to speak to different people. Her first book, *The Secret Language of Synchronicity*, is an exploration of these types of guiding messages.

Jenna continued her research (and collecting of more stories!), resulting in this book on how meaningful coincidence can guide our writing. She's learned there's always more to explore about the big U's symbols and signs, and would love to hear about your special experiences!

To see Jenna's other books go to her author's page here:
https://www.amazon.com/Jenna-Moore-Fuller/e/B018DDD0E8
You can also choose to "follow" her there if you like.

To hear about Jenna's future books, send an email to
jennamoorefullerbooks@gmail.com
Your email address will never be shared with anyone, period.

Thank you!